FROM PAIN TO PEACE

NAVIGATING RELATIONSHIPS AFTER TRAUMA

By Danyle Wilson

A Letter to Myself

I've been through pain that tried to break me, pain that came through betrayal, disappointment, and relationships that left lasting wounds. But I am still here. And the fact that I'm reading this now is proof that I'm not only surviving, I'm healing, growing, and becoming.

This book is more than just words on a page. It's a mirror, a map, and a mission. It reminds me that my healing is not just for me, it's for everyone connected to me. My peace will touch my family. My wholeness will impact my children and grandchildren. My healing will shape how I lead, how I love, how I show up in business, at work, and in ministry.

From this moment on, I give myself permission to keep growing, even when it feels slow or uncertain. I will revisit these pages as often as I need because true transformation requires repetition, reflection, and commitment. I'm not just reading to feel better; I'm reading to become better, for myself and for those I love.

I will have, build, and maintain healthy relationships, in my home, in the workplace, in business, with my family, children, grandchildren, friends, and my spouse. I will choose peace over patterns, communication over conflict, and love over fear. I will handle money with wisdom, honor my dreams with discipline, and walk in alignment with the visions God has placed in me.

I will no longer live from a place of reaction, but from a place of restoration. I will not let trauma lead my decisions.

Whatever age I was when the trauma occurred, I am no longer that age.

I now speak directly to that younger version of myself: *You were traumatized but I am not being traumatized anymore.* You no longer get to make decisions for me without my permission. You keep trying to choose trauma for me again and again dressed in different faces because you're afraid of being hurt again. But in doing so, you've only repeated the same pain in disguise.

I am no longer living under that fear. I am no longer being traumatized, and I am no longer you.

I commit to reminding the trauma of my younger self: *You are healing. You can no longer reveal your traumatic age or interrupt my present. You no longer get to dictate my today.*

Today, I am healed. I am no longer traumatized. And I will no longer allow my younger self shaped by trauma to run my life or deny me the future of peace that I deserve.

Instead, I'll respond with clarity, compassion, and conviction. I will protect my peace, set necessary boundaries, and choose connections that reflect who I am becoming.

The healing I'm choosing today will ripple into every area of my life. It will show up in the way I raise my children, the way I speak to my spouse, the way I steward opportunities, and the way I pursue my calling.

I am not just healing for the past I am healing for my future and everyone who will benefit from the healed version of me.

This book will remain close by not as a crutch, but as a companion. A tool I return to again and again until discipline becomes second nature, until my thought life is strong and peaceful, and until every relationship around me is rooted in truth, trust, and wholeness.

So I speak this over myself today: I will love boldly. I will forgive fully. I will lead with grace. And I will keep walking forward, from pain to peace one step, one moment, one decision at a time.

With deep love and renewed strength,

(Your Name)

Table of Contents

Navigating Connections After Trauma

Danyle Wilson is uniquely gifted with the ability to see beyond surface problems and uncover the deep-rooted issues that often guide people's lives without them even realizing it. She supports individuals, couples, and those on personal growth journeys, driven by a deep passion to help others grow and maintain a healthy life free from trauma. Having navigated these struggles herself, Danyle understands how the voice of trauma rooted in past wounds can quietly shape decisions, influence relationships, and distort one's sense of self-worth. Her heart is to help others break free from these patterns and step into a life of healing, purpose, and lasting emotional health.

The journey from pain to peace begins with understanding that betrayal does not have to define your future. If you're seeking tools to forgive, rebuild trust, and cultivate enduring connections, both spiritual and relational, without allowing past trauma to dictate your choices, you're in the right place. This book is designed to empower you to reclaim your life and make decisions rooted in faith, healing, and purpose rather than in the wounds of your past.

It's important to clarify from the outset that I'm not suggesting you will never face hardships or emotional pain. Life is full of trials, and the reality of human existence means that hurt is inevitable. However, this book will equip you with the tools to navigate those trials and break free from the strongholds of trauma that may have kept you stuck in a cycle of pain. You will learn the transformative power of forgiving quickly, which will allow your heart, deeply connected to your mind, to respond in healthier, more empowered ways. When your heart and mind align with new tools that transcend trauma, they will guide you toward victorious decision-making and a life of freedom.

Through the principles, insights, and strategies shared in these pages, you will discover how to break free from the cycle of pain and step into a life of wholeness and peace. Together, we will address the lingering effects of betrayal and dismantle its hold on your decisions, replacing it with clarity, restoration, and victory.

Throughout this book, you will also learn to identify the subtle yet profound ways trauma influences your thoughts, emotions, and choices. These deep-seated patterns often lead to repeated cycles of hurt in relationships, finances, mental health, and spiritual life. By developing a healthy thought life, a forgiving heart, and increased self-awareness, you'll acquire the tools needed to cultivate peace and purpose. No longer will trauma direct your path; healing will.

This is only the beginning of your journey. The road to healing may not always be smooth, but with every step forward, you'll begin to rewrite your story. It will require patience, persistence, and a commitment to growth, but it will absolutely be worth it. As you move through this process, my hope is that by the end of this book, you'll be empowered to transition from pain to peace. You'll find the strength to live a life filled with serenity, purpose, and power, no matter where you start. Healing is not just a destination. It is a transformation that unfolds one step at a time.

Are you ready to begin this life-changing journey?
Let's take the first step together.

CHAPTER 1

Breaking the Cycle: From Pain to Peace

This journey is about transitioning from a life defined by pain to one marked by peace. It's about learning how to respond to life's challenges in ways that empower you, rather than perpetuating cycles of hurt. One of the most important steps in this transformation is understanding the power of forgiveness specifically, learning to forgive quickly.

Forgiveness doesn't mean forgetting, excusing, or diminishing the wrongs that have been done to you. It doesn't mean that your pain isn't valid. Forgiveness, when practiced intentionally, frees your heart. And because your heart is deeply connected to your mind, the place from which your decisions and responses arise, it will begin to shift the way you interact with the world. The heart is more than just an emotional center; it is the wellspring from which your words and actions flow. As the Bible says, "Out of the abundance of the heart, the mouth speaks" (Matthew 12:34). By giving your heart new tools of peace rather than pain you begin to make healthier, more empowered choices.

You might be wondering, "But I've been carrying this hurt for so long. How can I just let it go?" The truth is that this process will take time. But it starts with a commitment to offer your heart new resources. The first step is understanding that trauma and pain have been shaping your decisions, often without your consent.

Let's be honest. If you're like most people, you may not seek professional help to process past trauma. Facing those wounds head-on can be difficult, and seeking therapy can feel overwhelming. But I want you to know that there is hope, and there is another way.

Danyle Wilson, a solutionist who has helped individuals, couples, and those on their journey to uncover the root causes of their struggles, often finds that many of her clients are unknowingly being guided by the voice of their trauma. This voice, which originates from past wounds, shapes their decisions, relationships, and even their sense of self-worth.

Through her work, Danyle discovered that sometimes the trauma people experience doesn't even belong to them directly. It can be part of a family's history what is known as bloodline trauma. Initially skeptical, Danyle's perspective shifted after reading *It Didn't Start With You* by Mark Wolynn. In his groundbreaking book, Wolynn describes how trauma can transcend generations. If a family member experiences a traumatic event at a specific age, that trauma may resurface when someone in the family reaches the same age. This isn't a coincidence. It's as if the emotional residue of trauma is passed down, unknowingly affecting family members. For instance, Wolynn shares a story of a man who had an irrational fear of being shot. He couldn't understand why this fear had taken root until he discovered that his grandfather had been shot in the arm at age 40. When the man turned 40, he began experiencing the same terror.

This phenomenon isn't limited to physical trauma. It can also involve deeply ingrained emotional responses passed down through generations. So, what does this mean for you on your journey from pain to peace? Simply put, some of the patterns you've been living with may not be entirely your own. They may be echoes of past wounds, inherited without your consent, yet deeply influencing the way you navigate your world.

Perhaps you find yourself caught in a cycle of self-destructive decisions or consistently choosing relationships that leave you feeling drained or unfulfilled. These patterns are not a reflection of who you truly are but rather a manifestation of trauma that has shaped your emotional responses over time.

The voice of pain speaks loudly, often without us realizing it. It influences our choices, our relationships, and even our self-perception. But here's the good news: that voice doesn't have to control your life. You can learn to recognize when trauma is making your decisions, and you can choose to stop letting it dictate your actions.

In many cases, this voice has been making decisions for you without your permission.

You might not even realize how often past hurts are shaping your present reality. Perhaps you've chosen friendships or romantic partners that mirror past wounds, or you find yourself reacting to everyday situations in ways that feel automatic, even though they no longer serve you. Trauma can hijack your ability to think clearly, causing you to act out of fear, insecurity, or unresolved hurt.

Now, let's pause for a moment and reflect on this powerful truth: your pain does not define your future.

This is the cycle of pain the emotional scars that never truly heal, continuously shaping the way you respond to life. But the cycle can be broken.

You don't have to stay stuck. It's time to take back control and start making decisions from a place of healing, not hurt. You deserve to experience peace, not just survival. It's possible to rewrite your story, shifting from reacting out of pain to responding with wisdom, strength, and peace.

One of the greatest misconceptions we carry is that pain defines us. We often identify with the wounds we've experienced, as if they become part of who we are. But here's the truth: your pain is not your identity. Pain may have been a chapter in your story, but it does not have to be the title of your life. When you release the grip of past hurts, you make space for peace, healing, and transformation. In the same way a broken heart can be mended, your past wounds can be healed through the power of forgiveness and intentional self-compassion.

The key to breaking this cycle lies in understanding the power of choice. Every day, you are presented with decisions, big and small, that shape your reality. The choices you make are rooted in the state of your heart and mind. When you allow trauma to continue influencing your decisions, you unknowingly hand over your power. But when you make the conscious decision to forgive, to release old pain, and to seek healing, you regain control over your life. Forgiveness becomes not just an emotional release but a deliberate choice to shift the direction of your life from the past to a future filled with peace.

Let's talk about the power of vulnerability. So often, we guard our pain, believing that showing it makes us weak or unworthy. But vulnerability is the birthplace of healing. The more we are willing to be open with ourselves, acknowledging the pain we carry, the more we allow the healing process to take root. It's only when we stop hiding from our pain that we can allow the process of forgiveness to begin. Vulnerability also opens the door to deeper, more authentic relationships. When we choose to be vulnerable with others, we give them permission to do the same. This shared experience of openness fosters mutual understanding and trust, which are essential for true healing.

Another key to breaking the cycle of pain is the practice of self-compassion. We tend to be our harshest critics, especially when we are in the midst of pain. We beat ourselves up for not healing fast enough, for making mistakes, or for still holding onto hurt. But healing takes time, and you deserve grace along the way. Self-compassion is the practice of treating yourself with the same love and kindness you would show to a dear friend in need. By offering yourself patience and understanding, you create an internal environment conducive to healing. The more compassionate you are with yourself, the more you can extend that same compassion to others.

Finally, it's essential to recognize that healing is a journey, not a destination. The path from pain to peace doesn't happen overnight, and there's no perfect way to heal. It's about taking consistent steps toward healing, embracing the discomfort of growth, and being gentle with yourself along the way. As you break free from the cycle of pain, you'll discover that each day brings new opportunities to choose peace, to practice forgiveness, and to build a life rooted in emotional freedom. It's a journey that requires persistence, courage, and the willingness to move forward even when it feels difficult. But with each step, you will move closer to the life you were meant to live, a life of peace, purpose, and joy.

Free from the Cycle

The time for change is now. You don't have to stay stuck. It's time to take back control and start making decisions from a place of healing, not hurt. You deserve to experience peace, not just survival. It's possible to rewrite your story, shifting from reacting out of pain to responding with wisdom and strength.

So, what's the next step? Start by recognizing the patterns in your life that have been shaped by trauma. Notice how it has influenced your decisions, relationships, and self-image. Then, commit to creating new tools for your heart tools of forgiveness, strength, and resilience. It's time to replace the voice of pain with the voice of peace.

Journal Exercises

- Write down the traumas you've identified that are obvious you want to turn from?

____

____

____

____

- Reflect on an area of your life where you feel trapped in a cycle of pain. What is the root of this cycle, and how has it influenced your decisions?

____

____

____

____

- Write down one specific decision you made recently that was shaped by past trauma. How would you choose differently if you made this decision from a place of peace and healing?

____

____

____

____

- Create a forgiveness list. Identify people, including yourself, whom you need to forgive. Write down one step you can take today to begin the process of forgiveness.

____

____

____

____

____

- Practice self-compassion today. Write a letter to yourself as if you were a dear friend, offering understanding and kindness.

____

____

____

____

____

Father God,

I come before You today with a heart full of gratitude and a longing for peace. I acknowledge the pain I've carried for so long, and I ask for Your help in breaking free from the cycle that has held me captive. I surrender my hurts, my fears, and my doubts to You. Heal my heart, Lord, and replace the wounds with Your peace.

I ask for Your strength to forgive those who have wronged me, including myself. Help me to release the past and make room for new growth and healing. Teach me to see myself as You see me worthy of love, compassion, and grace. I give You permission to transform the parts of me that have been shaped by pain and to replace them with Your truth and peace.

Lord, I trust that You are with me every step of this journey. When I feel weak, remind me of Your power. When I feel lost, guide me with Your wisdom. Help me to embrace the healing process, knowing that with You, all things are possible.

In the name of Jesus, I pray,

Amen.

CHAPTER 2

Understanding Trauma and Its Impact on Relationships

Defining Trauma and Its Various Forms: An In-Depth Exploration of Understanding and Overcoming Trauma

Trauma is not just an event; it is an emotional and psychological wound that can affect individuals long after the incident has passed. It results from distressing experiences like abuse, neglect, accidents, or loss, and its impact varies greatly. While some individuals find healing through time and support, others carry invisible scars that affect their thoughts, behaviors, and relationships for years. Trauma is not a one-size-fits-all experience. It manifests in different forms, shaping how people interact with themselves and the world around them.

I want you to take a moment and think about your life. Can you identify moments of pain that still influence your decisions today? Perhaps it's the weight of an abusive relationship, the sting of betrayal, or the ache of loss. These experiences don't just disappear with time. They become embedded in our emotional makeup, shaping how we navigate life. Trauma doesn't need to be something dramatic to affect you. It could be a subtle experience that, over time, affects your confidence or trust in others. Trauma can quietly take root in your heart and mind, and understanding its many forms helps you acknowledge that healing is possible.

There are several types of traumas, each with distinct characteristics and challenges. The three primary categories are:

Acute trauma: This form of trauma arises from a single overwhelming event. Examples include accidents, natural disasters, or violent encounters. While the emotional response to acute trauma can be intense, it may be temporary if proper support and coping mechanisms are in place.

Chronic trauma: This stems from prolonged exposure to distressing circumstances. It could be the result of ongoing abuse, living in an unsafe environment, or enduring long-term emotional or physical neglect. Unlike acute trauma, chronic trauma can leave long-lasting emotional scars and is often more difficult to overcome without intervention or the healing power of God.

Complex trauma: This involves repeated, multiple traumatic events, often beginning in childhood. This form of trauma can have the most profound effect on emotional and psychological development. The individual may grow up in an environment where they experience sustained harm and may struggle with lasting issues related to trust, identity, and self-worth.

Understanding these distinctions is crucial for recognizing how trauma manifests in both the individual and their relationships. For example, a person who has experienced chronic trauma may develop coping mechanisms that affect their behavior in relationships, often resulting in patterns of withdrawal or difficulty with emotional intimacy.

Trauma's impact extends far beyond the initial event. It can fundamentally alter emotional health and interfere with an individual's ability to engage in healthy relationships. Many individuals who have experienced trauma struggle with anxiety, depression, and a range of emotional regulation issues. These emotional challenges often spill over into relationships, creating significant barriers to intimacy, trust, and effective communication.

As you read through this, ask yourself: What have I allowed to define me? Are you allowing past hurt to steer your decisions today? It's important to recognize the impact of trauma not to relieve the pain, but to take back control over your life and healing. Naming the trauma, you've experienced, whether acute, chronic, or complex, is the first step in beginning to process it and move forward.

Psalm 147:3 (AMP) reminds us, "He heals the brokenhearted and binds up their wounds." This verse acknowledges that emotional pain is real and that healing is possible through divine intervention. Just as physical wounds need care, emotional wounds require attention, healing, and the right support.

Healing begins when you confront the reality of how trauma has shaped you. It's okay to acknowledge its presence in your life. In fact, it's necessary. So, what does it look like for you to acknowledge your trauma? Perhaps it's having an honest conversation with yourself, writing it out in a journal, or seeking help to process those wounds. Whatever it is, healing is a journey that requires awareness, understanding, and a willingness to step into the discomfort of facing what has hurt you.

How Trauma Affects Emotional Health and Relationships

The effects of trauma go beyond the initial experience, reshaping the way individuals process emotions and engage with others. Many survivors of trauma face ongoing battles with anxiety, depression, and difficulty regulating their emotions. These struggles often create barriers to healthy relationships. Trauma survivors may exhibit behaviors such as avoidance, hypersensitivity to conflict, or emotional shutdown, leaving them and their loved ones trapped in cycles of misunderstanding and frustration.

Have you ever felt like your emotions are on a roller coaster one minute feeling fine, and the next, overwhelmed by sadness or anger? Trauma can make you feel like you're living in a constant state of alertness or instability. You may find yourself reacting to situations in ways that don't match the moment, often feeling trapped in a cycle of emotional upheaval. This isn't because you're weak or incapable. It's a direct result of unresolved trauma that impacts how you process emotions. It's frustrating, and it can make you feel isolated or misunderstood, but you are not alone.

I want to remind you that it's okay to feel these things. It doesn't make you any less of a person. In fact, it's a sign that you've experienced something painful that is worthy of attention and care. You are not the sum of your emotional responses. Your heart is simply communicating that it needs healing. And with the right tools, support, and mindset, it's possible to regain emotional stability and rebuild trust in yourself and others.

Imagine for a moment being free from the constant emotional strain. Picture yourself reacting calmly, making decisions from a place of peace, and engaging in relationships without fear or hesitation. This isn't a far-off dream, it's a possibility within your reach. It takes time and work, but you can retrain your emotional responses. You have the power to rewrite how trauma has defined your emotions, and with that, begin to transform the way you relate to others.

The Role of the Mind in Healing from Trauma

Dr. Caroline Leaf, in her book *Who Switched Off My Brain?* delves into the scientific aspects of how trauma affects the brain. According to Dr. Leaf, unresolved trauma creates neurochemical imbalances in the brain, impairing one's ability to manage emotions effectively. These imbalances can result in emotionally toxic behavior that disrupts relationships. Without addressing these toxic thought patterns, individuals are likely to continue struggling with emotional dysregulation when the ability to control or manage emotions, behavior, or physical responses is compromised.

Dr. Leaf emphasizes the mind's power in overcoming trauma. Trauma becomes ingrained in our thought patterns, influencing how we perceive ourselves and the world. Toxic thought loops reinforce emotional pain, making healing seem out of reach. Over time, this mental conditioning fragments our thoughts, emotions, and behaviors, leaving us feeling misaligned.

To break free from this cycle, it is essential to focus on renewing the mind. Romans *12:2 (AMP) urges us, "Do not be conformed to this world, but be transformed by the renewing of your mind."* Transformation begins with changing how we think and process experiences. Healing from trauma involves recognizing harmful thought patterns and intentionally replacing them with healthier, more constructive thoughts. By doing so, individuals can begin to shift from a place of emotional numbness or pain to one of healing and hope.

In others, signs of trauma might appear as sudden emotional outbursts, social withdrawal, or difficulty expressing emotions. Understanding these symptoms and their root causes can help cultivate empathy and open the door for healing. Recognizing trauma in loved ones also provides an opportunity to offer support through active listening, compassion, and patience.

The Bible encourages us with the reminder that God deeply cares for us. *1 Peter 5:7 (AMP) states, "Cast all your cares on Him, for He cares for you."* This verse offers both comfort and a reminder that we don't need to carry our pain alone. Healing begins when we acknowledge our struggles and invite the healing power of God into our lives.

Have you ever found yourself stuck in a cycle of negative thinking? Maybe you catch yourself believing that things will never get better or that you'll always be trapped in pain. These thought patterns are often a result of trauma rewiring how we see the world and ourselves. But here's the good news: your mind is capable of healing. Just like a muscle, the more you practice new, positive thinking patterns, the stronger they become. The first step is recognizing that the negative thoughts don't define who you are, they are simply habits that can be changed.

Take a moment and reflect on the words you speak to yourself. Are they kind and encouraging, or do they echo the pain of past experiences? Your thoughts have the power to shape your emotions, and with practice, you can replace those harmful loops with affirmations of strength and resilience. It won't happen overnight, but as you begin to replace negative thinking with forward-focused thoughts, you'll start to see a shift in your emotional well-being.

It's normal to feel resistance to change, especially when the mind has been conditioned to believe certain lies. But trust me transformation is possible. By aligning your thoughts with truth, whether through prayer, affirmations, or positive self-talk, you can break the chains that trauma has placed around your mind. Imagine a future where you not only heal from your pain but grow stronger because of it.

Your mind is a powerful tool, and when you begin to nurture it with healing thoughts, you'll start to notice shifts in how you feel. Healing doesn't mean the trauma never happened. It means you've learned to respond to it differently. The more you choose to focus on thoughts that empower and uplift you, the more you'll begin to experience emotional freedom.

As we embark on the journey of healing from pain to peace, it's essential to recognize that emotional restoration requires more than just addressing the pain itself. It involves transforming the patterns of thought and belief that were shaped by those experiences. Often, these become intertwined with our pain, keeping us stuck in a loop of self-doubt, fear, and helplessness.

The Story of Job: A Biblical Perspective on Trauma

The story of Job offers a profound example of trauma, loss, and eventual restoration. Job suffered immensely, losing his children, wealth, and health, without understanding why. His grief led him to question everything. Yet, his story demonstrates that even in the darkest moments, healing and renewal are possible.

I want to share with you that, just like Job, your struggles do not define your worth. There may be seasons in life when everything feels like it's falling apart, and you may feel abandoned or overwhelmed. But Job's story is a testament to resilience and faith. It shows that no matter how deep the pain, there is always hope for restoration. Healing comes when we place our trust in God, believing that He is working in the midst of our pain, even when we don't understand the reasons.

When you face hardship, it's natural to question why things are happening. You might be in a season of deep pain right now, asking God why He allows you to suffer. But the key to Job's healing wasn't just understanding why it was trusting in God's sovereignty. Your healing might not look like an instant miracle, but it will come when you continue to lean on God, knowing that He can turn even the deepest wounds into something beautiful.

So, I encourage you to hold onto hope, even in your darkest moments. Remember that Job's restoration came in time, and so will yours. Your story is not over yet. Just like the tree in Job's vision, you too can sprout again, no matter how many times life has cut you down. Keep moving forward in faith, knowing that God is working in your life to heal, restore, and make you whole.

Recognizing the Signs of Trauma in Yourself and Others

Recognizing trauma in yourself or others is an essential step toward healing. Symptoms can be subtle or obvious, ranging from emotional numbness and anxiety to mood swings and intrusive flashbacks. Survivors may unconsciously avoid people, places, or situations that trigger painful memories, unintentionally isolating themselves from healing and growth.

Have you ever felt an overwhelming urge to avoid something or someone, even though you can't explain why? Or perhaps, there's a part of you that's always on edge, not fully able to relax or be present in the moment. These could be signs that trauma has been silently influencing your life. The mind and body often respond to past wounds in ways we don't immediately recognize, but when you begin to look for these signs, healing can begin.

Take a moment to check in with yourself. Are there things in your life that you've avoided or suppressed? Whether it's certain memories, relationships, or situations, trauma often causes us to retreat from what feels too painful to face. But recognizing this is the first step toward reclaiming your healing journey. You don't have to face it alone. Whether through therapy, spiritual guidance, or self-care practices, you can gradually process these memories and reclaim your power.

For those around you, trauma might manifest in ways that seem confusing. You may witness someone in your life pulling away emotionally or reacting in ways that seem disproportionate. Rather than judging or feeling frustrated, remember that trauma often leads to protective behaviors. If you can approach others with empathy and patience, you may help them open up to the possibility of healing. Just as you need compassion and understanding, so do they.

Healing begins when we recognize the signs of trauma, whether in ourselves or others. It is a process, but it's one that leads to emotional freedom, connection, and growth. Keep moving forward with compassion for yourself and those around you. The path to healing may not be easy, but it is always worth it.

Journal Exercises

Take some time to reflect on the key concepts covered in this chapter.

Journaling is a powerful tool for understanding and processing your emotions. As you move forward in your healing journey, use these prompts to guide your reflections and actions:

- Reflect on any experiences in your life that you consider traumatic. Write about how these events may have shaped your emotional responses and relationships.

____

____

____

____

____

- What forms of trauma have you experienced acute, chronic, or complex? How do you think these have impacted your emotional health and relationships?

____

____

____

____

____

- **This week, identify one specific traumatic event that has shaped your emotional responses.** Write a letter (that you won't send) to yourself about how that event affected your life. This will help you gain perspective and allow you to start processing the pain associated with it.

____

____

____

____

- **Pick one recurring negative thought and challenge it.** Write down a positive, truth-filled alternative to that thought. For instance, if you often think, *"I am not worthy,"* replace it with, *"I am a beloved child of God, created with purpose."* Write this affirmation on a sticky note and place it where you'll see it throughout the day.

____

____

____

____

- **Write a forgiveness letter to someone who has hurt you.** Express the pain you've felt but also choose to forgive them. You don't need to send the letter, but it's an important step toward freeing yourself from the emotional weight of unforgiveness.

- **Spend a few minutes each day visualizing yourself free from past pain and walking in emotional wholeness.** Picture yourself interacting with others with peace and confidence. Allow yourself to feel the relief and freedom that comes with this transformation. Write about the changes you notice in your thoughts and behaviors.

____

____

____

____

____

- **Choose one action step you can take this week to move forward in your healing process.** Write it down and commit to following through.

____

____

____

____

____

- **What is one practical step you can take this week to help renew your mind and emotions?** It could be a self-care action, seeking therapy, journaling, or engaging in a support system.

____

____

____

- **Commit to taking one small action this week that helps you heal emotionally.** It could be scheduling a therapy session, joining a support group, or practicing a relaxation technique like deep breathing. Write down the steps you will take and how it will contribute to your healing journey.

____

____

____

____

- **Take a moment to reflect on the small victories you've experienced this week** whether it's a shift in perspective, an action you've taken, or a moment of peace. Offer up a prayer of gratitude for those breakthroughs and ask God to continue healing you and guiding you toward emotional freedom.

____

____

____

____

- **Think about some of the negative thought patterns that have resulted from past trauma.** Journal about how these thoughts have affected your behaviors and decisions.

____

____

____

- **What are three recurring negative thoughts you've noticed in your life?** How have they shaped the way you interact with others and view yourself?

____

____

____

____

____

Scripture to Reflect On:

Matthew 12:34 (AMP) – *"For out of the fullness (the overflow, the superabundance) of the heart the mouth speaks."*

Consider how past trauma may have filled your heart with pain, and how healing can begin when you allow God to fill your heart with His peace.

Romans 12:2 (AMP) – *"And do not be conformed to this world (any longer with its superficial values and customs), but be transformed and progressively changed by the renewing of your mind..."*

Considering how renewing your mind is a vital step in transforming your thoughts and behaviors.

Ephesians 4:32 (AMP) – *"Be kind and helpful to one another, tenderhearted, forgiving one another, just as God in Christ also has forgiven you."*

Reflect on how forgiveness releases you from the burden of bitterness and opens your heart to healing.

Psalm 34:18 (AMP) – *"The Lord is near to the brokenhearted and saves those who are crushed in spirit."*

Take comfort in knowing that as you visualize your healing, God is near, bringing comfort and restoration.

Proverbs 4:23 (AMP) – *"Watch over your heart with all diligence, for from it flow the springs of life."*

Your healing is a process of diligently guarding your emotional health and making choices that align with God's will for your life.

Forgiveness and Emotional Healing

Consider the role forgiveness plays in your healing process. Is there someone including yourself, you need to forgive in order to move forward?

Who do you need to forgive, and what would it take for you to release that pain? How can you begin to heal by letting go of the past?

Visualization for Healing

Begin practicing the visualization technique. Picture yourself free from the emotional pain caused by trauma.

Write about what you see in your future how does it feel to be healed and whole?

Visualize yourself living a life of emotional freedom. What does that life look like? How does it feel to be in healthy, thriving relationships?

Gratitude and Prayer

End your journaling session with gratitude for any progress you've made and pray for continued healing.

Write down three things you are grateful for in your healing journey. Then, end with a prayer asking for God's healing and guidance in your transformation.

____

____

____

____

____

Prayer in Your Own Words

Prayer in Your Own Words

"Lord, I thank You for the healing that is taking place within me. I thank You for Your presence in every step of this journey. Please continue to guide my heart and mind as I walk through this process. I ask for Your wisdom and strength to break free from past pain and to embrace the freedom You've promised. In Jesus' name, Amen."

CHAPTER 3

Rewiring the Mind: Breaking the Cycle of Negative Thoughts

The mind is a powerful tool that governs not only our thoughts but also our beliefs, decisions, and actions. In particular, the cerebrum, the largest part of the brain, plays an essential role in regulating crucial functions such as movement, speech, intelligence, emotions, and sensory perception. While these functions may seem purely physical or intellectual, they deeply influence how we form beliefs, interpret the world around us, and shape our inner reality.

In this chapter, we will explore how the cerebrum profoundly affects belief systems and how we can harness its power to transform our thinking and, as a result, our lives.

Understanding the Cerebrum's Role in Belief Formation

The cerebrum is responsible for processing information from both our external environment and our internal thoughts. It influences belief formation through several key areas:

- *Sensory Perception:* **What We See and Hear**

Our cerebrum processes sensory information from the world around us, particularly visual and auditory stimuli. How we perceive the world shapes the foundation of our beliefs. For example, if you grow up in a supportive, loving environment, you are more likely to form positive beliefs about trust and relationships. However, if you are exposed to toxic relationships or unhealthy environments, your perceptions may lead you to believe that trust is difficult or unsafe.

This concept is supported by the Bible, which reminds us in Romans 12:2 (AMP), "Do not be conformed to this world any longer with its superficial values and customs, but be transformed and progressively changed by the renewing of your mind..." The renewing of the mind is an intentional process, one that shifts how we perceive the world and guides the formation of our beliefs.

- ***Emotions and Beliefs* (Read more about this in Chapter 4)**

Emotions significantly influence how we form beliefs. Our emotional responses to life events often dictate how we interpret those events and what we ultimately believe about ourselves, others, and the world. For example, trauma can lead to beliefs rooted in fear, distrust, and low self-worth. Conversely, positive emotional experiences can nurture beliefs of hope, optimism, and confidence.

According to the American Psychological Association (APA), emotion is defined as "a complex reaction pattern, involving experiential, behavioral, and physiological elements." Emotions are the way we process matters or situations that we find personally significant. They are not just feelings but intricate responses that shape how we experience the world around us. Emotional experiences consist of three components: subjective experience, a physiological and psychological response, and a behavioral or expressive response.

The subjective experience is how we consciously feel in a given moment, whether that is joy, sadness, fear, or any other emotion. The physiological response refers to the physical changes that occur within our bodies, such as an increased heart rate when we are anxious or the release of adrenaline when we are excited. The behavioral or expressive response is how we outwardly express what we feel, such as crying, laughing, or withdrawing from a situation.

Feelings emerge as a result of these emotional experiences, and because we are aware of them, they become something we can recognize, much like hunger or pain. Feeling is not the emotion itself, but its aftermath. That is the key. Our feelings, whether fleeting or intense, are shaped by various factors like memories, beliefs, and, importantly, our current emotional state. This is why it is crucial to be careful about how we speak or act when we are in the midst of strong emotions.

Emotions, by nature, are temporary. They are a passing sensation, an energy that surges through us in a moment. However, in that moment, the enemy often tries to exploit that feeling. It is in those vulnerable times when we feel most susceptible to self-doubt, anger, or despair. That is when the enemy whispers, "Now is the time. Let their emotions speak for them." Emotions can easily become the enemy's weapon. They can distort our reality and cause us to make decisions that may seem protective in the moment but, in truth, keep us from our destiny.

When we let emotional reactions take the lead, we risk speaking words that are not aligned with truth. In a heated moment, we may say things that tear down relationships, hurt others, or even worse damage our own self-belief. The enemy uses that. He plays on our emotions, making us feel abandoned by God, as though we are being punished or that God is not near to us in our suffering. The real danger is that it is our own words, driven by temporary emotions, that we later regret, thinking they were meant to protect us, but in reality, they have derailed us from the path of purpose.

Emotions, particularly those fueled by past trauma, have the power to make decisions for us without realizing it. We think we are guarding ourselves, protecting our hearts from harm, when we are keeping ourselves locked away from the very things we are meant to experience peace, growth, and fulfillment. Trauma-induced emotions often trick us into thinking they are helping us avoid future pain, when, in truth, they are preventing us from stepping into the future God has planned for us.

Dr. Caroline Leaf, in her book Who Switched Off My Brain? emphasizes how emotions can influence our thoughts and beliefs, stating, "Toxic thinking leads to toxic emotions. It's important to realize that your emotions are the result of what you think. The brain, emotions, and the body are interconnected, which means that your thoughts directly influence your feelings and behavior."

The Bible also acknowledges the connection between emotions and beliefs, offering comfort in times of emotional pain. Psalm 34:18 (AMP) reminds us, "The Lord is near to the brokenhearted and saves those who are crushed in spirit." This verse highlights how God understands our emotional pain and provides a path to healing.

- ***Cognitive Processing and Intelligence***

Cognitive functions such as reasoning, problem-solving, and critical thinking all reside in the cerebrum. These abilities enable us to evaluate and refine our beliefs. A person with strong critical thinking skills may challenge negative or harmful beliefs, whereas others may passively accept beliefs based on external influences or past experiences. Dr. Leaf's research underscores the importance of actively changing our thought patterns. She writes, "The thoughts you think repeatedly create the brain patterns that dictate your behavior. If you want to change your behavior, you must change your thought patterns." This concept aligns with the Bible's guidance to renew the mind and transform our thinking through Christ (Romans 12:2).

- ***Speech and Self-Talk***

The cerebrum is also responsible for the words we speak and our internal dialogue, or self-talk. This internal dialogue plays a crucial role in shaping our belief systems. Negative self-talk can reinforce beliefs of inadequacy, failure, and fear, while positive affirmations can build self-worth, confidence, and hope.

The Bible speaks to the power of words in Proverbs 18:21 (AMP), "Death and life are in the power of the tongue, and those who love it will eat its fruit." Our words have the power to shape our reality, and through positive self-talk, we can begin to reshape our beliefs for the better.

- ***Decision-Making and Actions***

Beliefs govern our decisions, and the cerebrum is at the center of this process. When we form a belief, it often influences the actions we take. For example, if you believe that success is only achieved through hard work and sacrifice, this belief may drive you to work tirelessly, sometimes to the detriment of your health or relationships. Conversely, if you believe that life can be balanced and fulfilling, you are more likely to make decisions that support your well-being and emotional health.

Dr. Leaf explains that beliefs formed in childhood and throughout life deeply influence our decision-making processes. She writes, "The brain is a complex network that stores information and memories, which influence our future decisions and actions. Trauma or stress can distort our memory and decision-making abilities.

The Hidden Consequences of Trauma: A Case Study in Belief Formation

Let us take a closer look at how early trauma can shape beliefs and influence decisions later in life. Imagine a person who grew up in a household of financial instability. Perhaps they faced constant financial struggles, rationing food, and witnessing persistent tension and stress due to money problems. These experiences shaped their belief system: money equals security, and financial instability equals failure.

Now, as an adult, this person may have developed a relentless drive to work and earn as much as possible, hoping to avoid the hardships they experienced in childhood. While this drive may yield professional success, it often comes at a high emotional cost. The individual may neglect personal relationships, become emotionally distant from their spouse or children, and prioritize work over family, believing that financial success is the ultimate measure of security.

However, in their subconscious, the belief that financial stability equates to security has also led to emotional instability. The person has inadvertently become consumed by the pursuit of financial success, causing a neglect of emotional health and familial connections. What was once a protective belief has now become a limiting belief.

This cycle is often a result of trauma that has shaped the cerebrum's decision-making process. As Dr. Leaf explains, "Trauma can cause the brain to develop protective mechanisms that create survival-based beliefs. These beliefs, while initially helpful in avoiding further harm, can limit personal growth and affect relationships."

How Trauma Alters the Cerebrum and Belief Systems

Trauma can significantly alter the functioning of the cerebrum, particularly in the way beliefs are formed and processed. When trauma occurs, the brain often develops protective mechanisms designed to help the individual survive future threats. However, these protective beliefs often rooted in fear, distrust, and shame can hinder personal growth and emotional well-being.

For example, trauma can lead to heightened fear and hypervigilance. Someone who has experienced betrayal may develop a belief that no one can be trusted, as the brain is wired to protect them from further harm. Similarly, emotional trauma can result in a belief that no one can be trusted or lead to a sense of inadequacy or low self-worth, especially if negative self-talk becomes ingrained in the cerebrum's neural pathways.

The Bible speaks to this idea of emotional renewal, encouraging us to cast off old, limiting beliefs and embrace new, life-giving truths. 2 Corinthians 5:17 (AMP) declares, "Therefore, if anyone is in Christ, he is a new creature; the old things passed away; behold, new things have come." Healing from trauma requires not only the transformation of our thoughts but also the renewal of our belief systems in alignment with God's truth.

Harnessing the Power of the Mind: Rewriting Your Beliefs

The good news is that the cerebrum is not static. It is adaptable and capable of change. Neuroplasticity, the brain's ability to form new pathways, offers us hope. We can consciously reshape our beliefs and transform our lives by engaging in practices that promote emotional regulation, positive self-talk, mindfulness, and exposure to new experiences. Dr. Leaf provides several strategies for harnessing the power of the mind and reshaping beliefs:

- ***Positive Self-Talk and Repetition***: Regularly practicing positive affirmations and challenging negative thought patterns helps rewire the brain. Dr. Leaf explains, "The brain responds to repeated thought patterns. By changing our self-talk, we can reshape our beliefs and alter our behavior."

- ***Mindfulness and Emotional Regulation***: By engaging in mindfulness practices, we can learn to recognize and manage our emotions. This helps us avoid reacting impulsively to negative beliefs and emotions. Proverbs 16:32 (AMP) offers wisdom in this area: "He who is slow to anger is better than the mighty; he who rules his spirit than he who captures a city."

- ***Exposure to Positive Experiences:*** Actively seeking new, positive experiences and surrounding ourselves with supportive environments can challenge ingrained negative beliefs. The Bible encourages us to "set our minds on things above, not on earthly things" (Colossians 3:2, AMP), emphasizing the importance of focusing on positive and uplifting influences.

- ***Forgiveness and Healing:*** Forgiveness is a powerful tool for breaking free from the beliefs formed by trauma. As Dr. Leaf notes, "Forgiveness is one of the most powerful ways to release toxic beliefs and emotional pain."

Transforming Your Reality Through the Power of the Mind

The cerebrum plays a pivotal role in shaping our belief systems and, consequently, our actions. By understanding the brain's capacity to adapt and change, we can take proactive steps to transform our beliefs and create a life filled with hope, peace, and purpose. Healing from trauma is possible, and by harnessing the power of the mind, we can rewrite our stories, align our beliefs with God's truth, and live with greater clarity, strength, and joy.

As Dr. Leaf so aptly puts it, "The power of the mind is incredible. Through the renewing of our minds, we have the power to change our thoughts, our emotions, and our reality." And as we align our beliefs with God's Word, we can find healing, restoration, and the courage to live out our true purpose.

Recognizing the brain's ability to transform and heal is just the beginning. As we continue on this journey, it is essential to understand how our emotions and beliefs intertwine, shaping our responses to life's challenges. In the next chapter, we will explore the influence of emotions on beliefs, uncovering how our emotional experiences can form the foundation of our beliefs, and how shifting these patterns can lead to profound healing and growth.

Rewiring the Brain for Healing: Transforming the Mind

Healing from trauma is not merely an emotional process; it is a profound transformation that begins in the mind. The cerebrum, the powerhouse of the brain, plays a pivotal role in this change. It shapes how we perceive the world and ourselves. When trauma strikes, it forms harmful neural pathways that perpetuate negative beliefs, such as "I'm not good enough" or "I'm unworthy of love," creating a cycle that influences our actions, thoughts, and relationships. Here is the good news: your brain has an incredible ability to heal itself. This phenomenon, called neuroplasticity, allows you to rewire your brain by consciously shifting your thoughts.

In this journey of healing, you will not only let go of old, harmful patterns, but you will also embrace a new, empowered way of thinking that aligns with God's truth. Your thoughts, once distorted by trauma, will be replaced with affirmations of peace, love, and restoration. This is the beauty of healing: it is a process of reprogramming your brain and reclaiming the life you were always meant to live.

The Power of Neuroplasticity: Rewiring Your Beliefs

Healing begins in the mind, and your brain is more than capable of transformation. Neuroplasticity means that, with consistent effort, you can break free from old thought patterns and create new pathways for healing. The beliefs formed during trauma do not define who you are they are simply the result of painful experiences. Through positive reinforcement, affirmation, and emotional regulation, you can rewire your cerebrum to embrace God's truth about you.

Every time you practice affirmations, you are building a new neural pathway. These pathways become stronger with repetition, eventually replacing the old patterns of fear and self-doubt. This is the essence of healing: replacing lies with truth and forming new beliefs that align with the peace God offers.

Empowering Your Mind

In Pain to Peace, you will find visual prompts that are designed not just to be seen, but to inspire deep, lasting transformation. These tools work in tandem with the mind's healing process, helping you actively reprogram your brain for success.

- **Affirmation Cards: Replacing Lies with Truth**

Begin your healing journey each day by declaring powerful affirmations that challenge the false beliefs trauma has instilled in you. These cards serve as constant reminders of your true identity in Christ.

Example Affirmation: "I am worthy of love, peace, and abundance. I release the past and embrace the healing God has for me."

Write your affirmation on an index card, sticky note, or in your journal. Place it somewhere you will see it often, and each time you do, say it aloud with conviction. Visualize it sinking into your mind, becoming part of your new belief system.

- **Mindfulness Prompts: Anchoring in the Present**

Trauma often takes us out of the present moment, anchoring us in past pain. Mindfulness helps us return to the here and now, releasing overwhelming emotions and cultivating inner peace.

Mindfulness Prompt: "Right here, right now, I am safe. I release all fears and embrace peace."

When stress or negative thoughts arise, take a moment to pause. Focus on your breath. Inhale peace, exhale fear. Practice this for 3-5 minutes and notice how it grounds you in the present moment.

- **Brain Plasticity Visuals: Understanding Your Brain's Power**

Brain Plasticity is the process of rewiring your brain and visualizing it can make this transformation more tangible. Visual aids can help you understand that healing is not just about emotional recovery it is a biological process that brings lasting change.

Picture the brain's neural pathways. Some are old and tangled with negative beliefs, while others are fresh and vibrant with healing. Over time, the new pathways grow, and the old ones diminish.

One of the most powerful tools you can use is visualization. It allows you to see the transformation of your mind, replacing old trauma-based beliefs with peace-filled, empowering truths.

"Imagine a tangled mess of dark neural pathways in your brain, representing negative thoughts and beliefs. Now, see golden threads of light forming new, healthy pathways. These bright connections represent healing, trust, and peace. With each affirmation you speak and each positive thought you hold, these golden pathways grow stronger."

Keep this visual on hand, and as you practice mindfulness, affirmations, and visualization, imagine the new neural pathways forming and strengthening. You are literally reshaping your brain for healing.

Set aside time each day to practice this visualization. Visualize the new neural pathways forming and feel the peace that comes with each step forward. Allow your mind to fully embrace this new belief system rooted in truth, peace, and God's love.

Building New Beliefs with Consistency

Rewiring your brain takes time and commitment. Consistency is key. Each affirmation, each mindfulness practice, and each prayer builds upon the last, gradually changing your belief system from one of fear and pain to one of peace and truth.

Remember, the brain is like a garden. As Dr. Caroline Leaf says, "What you plant, water, and nurture will grow." So, as you nurture thoughts of peace, healing, and God's love, these beliefs will become your reality.

Journal Exercises

1. Morning Reflection & Affirmation

- *Begin your day with intentional reflection. Write down any negative thoughts or self-doubt.*

- *Replace each negative thought with a positive affirmation that aligns with the person you are becoming.*

- *Example: Instead of "I am not enough," say, "I am fearfully and wonderfully made, equipped for my purpose." (Psalm 139:14 AMP)*

2. Visualization & Gratitude Practice

- *Spend 5-10 minutes visualizing yourself living free from the weight of past experiences. - Picture the best version of yourself, walking in confidence and purpose.*

- *Write down three things you are grateful for to shift your focus from pain to progress. (1 Thessalonians 5:18 AMP – 'in every situation [no matter what the circumstances] be thankful and continually give thanks to God; for this is the will of God for you in Christ Jesus.')*

____

____

____

____

3. Rewriting the Narrative

- *Take a journal and rewrite a painful past experience from a victorious perspective.*

____

____

____

____

- *Acknowledge the lesson in the pain, and write a new belief that replaces the old wound.*
- *Example: "I was abandoned, which made me feel unworthy" → "I am worthy of love, and I choose to surround myself with those who see my value." (Jeremiah 29:11 AMP 'For I know the plans and thoughts that I have for you,' says the Lord, 'plans for peace and well-being and not for disaster, to give you a future and a hope.')*

____

____

____

____

4. Intentional Speech & Word Shaping

- *Pay attention to the words you speak throughout the day.*
- *If you catch yourself speaking negatively about yourself or your situation, stop and reframe it in a way that empowers growth and healing.*
- *Example: Instead of "I always fail," say, "Every experience is teaching me, and I am learning and improving." (Proverbs 18:21 AMP –*

'Death and life are in the power of the tongue, and those who love it and indulge it will eat its fruit and bear the consequences of their words.')

5. Evening Reflection & Release

- *Before bed, take a few moments to reflect on how you responded to challenges that day.*

- *Release any lingering negativity through deep breathing and a short prayer or meditation.*

- *Write down one belief you reinforced today and one area you will continue working on tomorrow. (Philippians 4:8 AMP – 'Finally, believers, whatever is true, whatever is honorable and worthy of respect, whatever is right and confirmed by God's word, whatever is pure and wholesome, whatever is lovely and brings peace, whatever is admirable and of good repute; if there is any excellence, if there is anything worthy of praise, think continually on these things [center your mind on them, and implant them in your heart].')*

Quote for the Day:

*"Do not be conformed to this world [any longer with its superficial values and customs], but be transformed and progressively changed [as you mature spiritually] by the renewing of your mind [focusing on godly values and ethical attitudes], so that you may prove [for yourselves] what the will of God is, that which is good and acceptable and perfect [in His plan and purpose for you]."
– Romans 12:2 AMP*

Heavenly Father, I surrender my thoughts and my heart to You today. Help me to replace every negative belief with Your truth. Strengthen me to see myself through Your eyes and to walk in the confidence of who You created me to be. Let my words align with Your promises, and may my mind be renewed daily by Your Word. In Jesus' name, Amen.

By consistently implementing these steps, you will begin to tear down the strongholds of past pain and build a mindset that aligns with the truth of who you are. True transformation takes daily practice, but with time, your new belief systems will become second nature, leading you to walk in freedom and confidence.

CHAPTER 4

The Influence of Emotions on Beliefs: Understanding the Connection

Emotions are powerful forces that shape our thoughts, beliefs, and ultimately, our lives. They play a central role in how we interpret our experiences and form our belief systems. Whether positive or negative, our emotional responses significantly influence how we view ourselves, others, and the world around us. This connection between emotions and beliefs is crucial to understanding how trauma can profoundly shape our internal world.

For instance, trauma whether caused by loss, betrayal, or abuse can give rise to beliefs rooted in fear, distrust, and low self-worth. These beliefs can affect all areas of life, creating barriers to personal growth, healthy relationships, and emotional well-being. In contrast, positive emotional experiences such as love, support, and validation can nurture beliefs of hope, optimism, and confidence. In this way, our emotions do not simply reflect what we experience; they actively shape how we interpret those experiences and the beliefs that emerge from them.

The Complex Nature of Emotions

Emotions are our internal responses to things that are personally significant. They affect us in three major ways:

- A Subjective Experience: This is how we consciously feel and perceive our emotional state.

- A Physiological Response: These are the physical changes we experience when we feel emotions like a racing heart during fear or tears when we're sad.

- A Behavioral or Expressive Response: This is how we act out our emotions, whether through crying, laughing, or withdrawing from others.

Feelings are a direct result of emotional experiences. Whether we feel joy, sadness, anger, or fear, we feel the aftermath of an emotion. Though these feelings may be temporary, their influence on our beliefs can be long-lasting. This is why we must be mindful of how we respond to emotions, particularly when they run high. As the Bible reminds us in James 1:19 (AMP), "Everyone must be quick to hear, slow to speak, and slow to anger."

Our emotions, when left unchecked, can lead us to impulsive decisions that we may later regret. It is in these moments that our words, shaped by fleeting emotions, can be twisted by the enemy to distort our reality.

The Power of Emotional Responses in Decision-Making

When we allow our emotions to govern us, we risk making decisions that pull us further from our true purpose or destiny. Trauma, for example, can stir up intense emotional reactions that cloud our judgment. These emotions, which may have once served as protective mechanisms, often trap us in patterns of fear and self-doubt, preventing us from embracing our potential. In these moments, we may believe we're making choices to safeguard ourselves, but in reality, we may be blocking our healing and growth.

This is where faith plays a crucial role. The Bible teaches that faith is the assurance of things hoped for, the conviction of things not seen (Hebrews 11:1). But faith is not merely believing in what we cannot see. It is deeply connected to how we feel and think. As Matthew Henry writes in his commentary, "Faith, like a living principle, is to be exercised in all our affections and passions… it governs the mind, overcomes the temptations of the world, and strengthens us in the face of life's adversities."

When we let emotions especially those shaped by past trauma

dictate our choices, we operate from a place of fear rather than faith. Faith, however, urges us to look beyond our immediate emotional state, trusting in God's promises even when everything around us feels overwhelming. Emotions rooted in trauma, such as fear and shame, can distort our beliefs, making us feel unworthy of healing or love. But faith empowers us to challenge those emotional distortions, holding firm to the truth that we are loved, accepted, and capable of overcoming.

Recognizing the impact of emotions on our beliefs and decisions is crucial, but it is only one piece of the healing puzzle. The key to breaking free from these emotional cycles lies in forgiveness. Forgiveness is a pathway to healing, allowing us to release the emotional grip of past wounds. As we move from holding onto hurt to offering forgiveness, we begin to dismantle the toxic beliefs and emotional responses that keep us stuck, making room for restoration and renewal. As Matthew Henry further notes, "Forgiveness is not just an act of releasing another person it is a step of faith, a declaration that you trust God to handle the wrongs and the hurt."

Embracing the Power of Forgiveness: In the next chapter, we will explore the transformative power of forgiveness and how it becomes the key to turning emotional pain into freedom. Forgiveness helps us walk boldly in our God-given purpose, moving from pain to peace.

Remember: Healing is not just about what we feel in the moment. It is about choosing to rise above those feelings, align our thoughts with God's truth, and reclaim the beliefs that bring us peace and purpose.

"Emotions may sway the soul, but faith anchors the heart."
– Danyle Wilson

Journal Exercises

Emotional Flowchart: Understanding How Emotions Shape Beliefs

Step 1: Emotion (e.g., Fear, Anger, Joy)

Step 2: Emotional Response (e.g., Racing Heart, Tears, Smile)

Step 3: Belief System (e.g., "I am unsafe," "I am loved," "I am worthy")

Step 4: Action or Reaction (e.g., Withdrawal, Speaking out, Reaching out)

Use this flowchart to map out how certain emotions influence the way you view the world and make decisions.

Identifying Emotional Triggers and Beliefs

- *Write down a recent emotional experience that had a strong impact on you (positive or negative).*

____

____

____

____

- *Identify the emotion: What emotion did you feel at the time? Was it fear, anger, sadness, or joy?*

____

____

____

____

- *Trace the belief formed: How did this emotion shape your belief about yourself, others, or the world?*

____

____

____

____

- *Notice the action taken: Did the emotion cause you to react impulsively or make a deliberate choice?*

____

____

____

____

By identifying the connection between emotions, beliefs, and actions, you'll gain insight into your emotional triggers and how they influence your decision-making.

- *Write about a time when an emotional reaction shaped your belief or led to a decision that was later regretted. How did that belief hold you back?*

____

____

____

____

- *Now, think about a time when your emotions were aligned with your faith and helped you make a decision that moved you closer to your purpose. How did your belief system guide you?*

____

____

____

____

Write the following in your journal

"I believe that my emotions do not define my destiny. Through faith, I can choose how to respond and reshape the beliefs that limit me."

____

____

____

____

- *"What belief have I been holding onto because of past emotional wounds? I choose to release this belief today."*

____

____

____

____

Next Steps: Visualize Healing and Freedom

Close your eyes and take a few deep breaths. Visualize yourself standing in a field of peace, where your past emotional wounds have been washed away. See yourself moving forward with faith, empowered by forgiveness and healed from the emotional grip of trauma. Picture the belief that once held you back transforming into a new belief rooted in hope, strength, and confidence. You are free to move forward.

Reflection for Today

Write down three beliefs you want to replace and pray over them. Example: "I replace the belief that 'I am unworthy of love' with the truth that 'I am loved and accepted by God.'"

____

____

____

____

Thank You for Your love and grace. I acknowledge that my emotions, though powerful, do not define who I am. I come before You today, asking for the strength to release the emotional pain of my past. Help me to forgive those who have hurt me, and most importantly, help me to forgive myself.

Let Your truth transforms my beliefs, replacing fear with faith, shame with self-worth, and doubt with confidence. Guide me as I take steps toward healing, believing that with You, all things are possible.

In Jesus' name, Amen.

CHAPTER 5

From Hurt to Hope: Forgiveness as a Healing Balm

The Importance of Forgiveness in the Healing Process

Forgiveness is one of the most powerful and transformative forces in the journey of emotional healing. It is an act of releasing emotional burdens and freeing ourselves from the chains of bitterness, anger, and pain that often stem from traumatic experiences. However, forgiveness is not always an easy or straightforward process. It challenges us to let go of what has hurt us, to release the hold that resentment and unforgiveness have on our hearts, and to move forward with emotional freedom.

In the aftermath of trauma, whether from betrayal, loss, abuse, or injustice, the emotional wounds can be deep and lasting. These wounds often fuel anger and bitterness, shaping the way we view ourselves, others, and even God. While emotional pain is a natural reaction to trauma, the decision to hold onto that pain can cause long-term damage to our mental, physical, and spiritual well-being. The act of forgiveness, however, offers a pathway to emotional healing and restoration.

The Biblical Perspective on Forgiveness

The story of Job in the Bible exemplifies the power of forgiveness and restoration. Job, a man who was upright and faithful to God, lost everything: his family, his wealth, and his health. His suffering was immense, and he endured accusations and judgments from his friends. Despite his anguish, Job did not curse God or give in to bitterness. Instead, he remained steadfast, and in time, God restored him, blessing him with twice as much as he had before.

Job 42:10 (AMP) states, *"The Lord restored the fortunes of Job when he prayed for his friends, and the Lord gave Job twice as much as he had before."* This passage highlights an essential truth. Healing and restoration often come through the act of releasing pain and embracing forgiveness. Job's story serves as a reminder that even in our deepest suffering, God has the power to bring us into a place of peace and abundance.

Job's story also teaches us about surrendering to God's plan. **Job 1:21 (AMP)** states, *"He said, 'Naked [without possession] I came into this world from my mother's womb, and naked I will return there. The Lord gave and the Lord has taken away; blessed be the name of the Lord.'"* This verse illustrates Job's ability to trust God despite his suffering. Trusting God is a crucial part of the forgiveness process because it involves letting go and allowing Him to work in our lives.

Additionally, **Job 42:7–8 (AMP)** says, *"After the Lord had spoken these words to Job, He said to Eliphaz the Temanite, 'My wrath is kindled against you and against your two friends because you have not spoken of Me what is right, as My servant Job has. Now therefore, take for yourselves seven bulls and seven rams, and go to My servant Job, and offer up a burnt offering for yourselves, and My servant Job will pray for you. For I will accept his prayer so that I may not deal with you according to your foolishness.'"*

This passage underscores the power of intercession. Job's act of praying for those who wronged him was directly tied to his own restoration.

Finally, Job 42:12 (AMP) states, *"The Lord blessed the latter days of Job more than his beginning; for he had fourteen thousand sheep, six thousand camels, a thousand yoke of oxen, and a thousand female donkeys."* This reinforces the message that God not only RESTORES but MULTIPLIES blessings when we choose to trust Him in our suffering, let go of bitterness, and walk in forgiveness.

What is Forgiveness?

Forgiveness is often misunderstood as merely excusing someone's harmful actions or letting them off the hook for their wrongdoings. However, true forgiveness is much more than that. Forgiveness is the voluntary choice to release the desire for retribution and revenge against those who have wronged us. It is a decision to release the hold that bitterness and resentment have over our hearts and minds.

John Bevere, in his book *The Bait of Satan*, argues that unforgiveness is like a trap that keeps us ensnared in a cycle of pain and bitterness. He writes, *"Offense is the bait of Satan, designed to keep us in bondage."* When we choose not to forgive, we allow the offense to dictate our emotional and spiritual state, giving the enemy an opportunity to use our pain to drive a wedge between us and our healing. Bevere emphasizes that forgiveness is not for the person who hurt us—it is for our own freedom and peace of mind.

Forgiveness is not about excusing harmful behavior or allowing someone to continue abuse or mistreating us. Instead, it is about releasing the emotional grip that the offense has on us so that we can heal and move forward. In this sense, forgiveness is an act of self-care and self-liberation.

Why is Forgiveness So Important?

The importance of forgiveness cannot be overstated. Myles Munroe, a renowned author and speaker, elaborates on the power of forgiveness, emphasizing that it is essential for both our emotional health and our spiritual well-being. Munroe teaches that unforgiveness is like poison to the soul. He writes, ***Unforgiveness is a weight that can be felt in every area of life physically, emotionally, and spiritually. It is the spiritual and emotional equivalent of carrying around a heavy burden that you were never meant to carry.***

When we refuse to forgive, we remain chained to the past. The hurt, betrayal, or trauma we experienced continues to dictate our emotions and decisions. Unforgiveness keeps us trapped in negative thought patterns, reinforcing feelings of inadequacy, fear, and distrust. This cycle can prevent us from experiencing the peace and joy that God desires for us.

The Bible makes it clear that forgiveness is not optional it is a command.

Matthew 6:14–15 (AMP) says, *"For if you forgive others their trespasses, [their reckless and willful sins], your heavenly Father will also forgive you. But if you do not forgive others, nurturing your hurt and anger with the result that it interferes with your relationship with God, then your Father will not forgive your trespasses."*

God's forgiveness of us is directly tied to our willingness to forgive others. This connection highlights the gravity of forgiveness, not only as a means of emotional healing but also as a requirement for spiritual restoration. When we hold onto unforgiveness, we allow the enemy to gain a foothold in our hearts, making it harder for us to experience God's grace and mercy.

What Happens When We Don't Forgive?

When we choose not to forgive, we subject ourselves to emotional and spiritual consequences. Unforgiveness can lead to resentment, bitterness, anger, and even physical illness. Research has shown that harboring unforgiveness is linked to increased stress, anxiety, depression, and chronic health problems. Emotionally, we become weighed down by the pain and resentment we carry, preventing us from living freely and joyfully.

Spiritually, unforgiveness separates us from God's grace. Jesus clearly teaches that God will not forgive our sins if we do not forgive others (Matthew 6:14–15). Unforgiveness creates a barrier between us and the fullness of God's love, preventing us from experiencing the healing and restoration He offers. Job's story teaches us that even after deep suffering,

God is faithful to restore us. When we choose forgiveness, we open the door for God to bring healing, renewal, and even double restoration, just as He did for Job.

What Happens After We Have Forgiven?

Forgiveness is not the end of the journey. It is the beginning of a new chapter. Once we forgive, we make space for healing, peace, and restoration. The weight that once held us back is lifted, allowing us to embrace new opportunities for growth and deeper relationships. We find freedom in knowing that our past no longer has control over our emotions or decisions.

When we truly forgive, we also create room for God to work in our lives. We begin to experience His love more deeply, and our hearts become more receptive to His guidance. Our relationships improve as we approach others with a spirit of grace rather than resentment. The peace that follows forgiveness is a testament to God's transformative power at work within us.

Journal

Heavenly Father,

I come before You with a heart that longs to be free from the weight of unforgiveness. I surrender my pain, my hurt, and my anger to You. Help me to release those who have wronged me, just as You have forgiven me. Give me strength to walk in love, even when it feels difficult. I trust in Your healing power and invite Your peace to fill my heart.

In Jesus' name, Amen.

- What areas of your life still hold the weight of unforgiveness?

____

____

____

____

- How has holding onto pain affected your emotional and spiritual well-being?

____

____

____

____

- What steps can you take today to begin releasing past hurts?

Visual Prompts & Exercises

- **Mindful Visualization:** Picture yourself releasing your pain to God, allowing Him to replace it with peace.

- **Forgiveness Letter:** Write a letter to someone you need to forgive (you don't have to send it) expressing your feelings and your decision to let go.

- **Commit to a daily affirmation:** I am free, I am whole, I choose peace.

- Create a small act of kindness for someone as a step toward emotional healing.

Reflection:

List three blessings in your life that unforgiveness has been blocking you from fully appreciating.

____

____

____

- What areas of your life still carry the burden of unforgiveness?

  ____

  ____

  ____

- How has holding onto pain shaped your emotional and spiritual journey?

  ____

  ____

  ____

  ____

- What is one step you can take today to begin releasing that pain?

  ____

  ____

  ____

  ____

Choose one person you can extend grace to today, even in a small way whether through kind words, a prayer, or a peaceful mindset.

If possible, perform a symbolic act to represent letting go such as tearing up a written grievance, lighting a candle, or stepping outside to take a deep breath and exhale your burdens.

Speak a short prayer, asking God to help you release the weight of unforgiveness from your heart.

Myles Munroe once said, "Unforgiveness is a weight that can be felt in every area of life physically, emotionally, and spiritually..."

Heavenly Father,

Thank You for the gift of forgiveness. I come before You with a heart that longs to be free from the weight of past hurts. Help me to surrender my pain and release those who have wronged me. Fill me with Your love and grace, and let peace replace every wound. I trust in Your healing power and choose to walk in the freedom of forgiveness.

In Jesus' name, Amen.

CHAPTER 6

Building Healthy Boundaries:

The Role of Boundaries in Maintaining Healthy Relationships

Boundaries are the invisible lines that define where one person ends and another begins. They are essential for moving from pain to peace in our relationships, helping individuals communicate their needs, preferences, and limits while ensuring mutual respect. By establishing clear boundaries, people can cultivate trust and safety, creating an environment where both parties can thrive. Healthy boundaries foster peace by facilitating open communication and allowing for honest dialogue about expectations and feelings. Ultimately, they play a critical role in preventing misunderstandings and conflicts, transforming pain into harmony and contributing to a more balanced relationship dynamic.

In a world where personal connections often feel strained or misunderstood, boundaries act as the foundation for meaningful relationships. Without them, even the strongest bonds can become fragile, weighed down by unmet expectations or unspoken frustrations. Boundaries are not barriers to intimacy but bridges that foster understanding, allowing *pain* to dissolve and *peace* to flow. They preserve individual identity while promoting connection. Boundaries are the cornerstone of relationships built on mutual respect and authenticity, creating a space where individuals can coexist without losing themselves.

As **Proverbs 4:23 (AMP)** reminds us, *"Watch over your heart with all diligence, for from it flow the springs of life."* Boundaries protect the heart, ensuring it remains a source of life and not a reservoir of unresolved pain. Likewise, **Job 11:18 (AMP)** encourages, *"Then you would trust [with confidence], because there is hope; you would look around you and rest securely."* Setting boundaries allows us to rest securely in the relationships God intends for us.

How Trauma Can Blur Boundaries and Lead to Unhealthy Dynamics

Trauma has the power to distort the perception of boundaries, often leaving individuals feeling exposed, vulnerable, and unable to protect themselves from further harm. For those who have experienced trauma, recognizing personal needs and asserting boundaries becomes challenging. This can manifest in various ways, such as overextending oneself to avoid conflict, tolerating disrespect out of fear, or feeling guilty when attempting to say no. These blurred boundaries can create unhealthy dynamics, often leading to cycles of pain that prevent the experience of lasting peace.

Trauma survivors may internalize the belief that their worth is tied to pleasing others or avoiding conflict. This often leads them to suppress their own needs to maintain relationships, even at the cost of their wellbeing. For instance, someone who has experienced abandonment may overcommit to ensure they are not left behind again, even though it results in emotional burnout or resentment. Similarly, a history of emotional abuse can lead individuals to question their right to set limits, fearing rejection or further harm. These behaviors keep them trapped in cycles of pain instead of allowing space for healing and peace.

Understanding the impact of trauma on boundaries is a crucial step toward healing. By recognizing how trauma distorts boundaries, individuals can begin to reclaim their autonomy and move from *pain to peace*. Rebuilding boundaries starts with acknowledging that personal needs and limits are valid, no matter what past experiences may suggest. This journey often involves unlearning unhealthy habits, addressing fears, and developing the confidence to assert oneself.

As **Psalm 34:18 (AMP)** assures us, *"The Lord is near to the heartbroken and He saves those who are crushed in spirit."* This verse reminds us that healing is possible, and through setting healthy boundaries, we can move from pain to peace.

Practical Steps for Establishing and Maintaining Effective Boundaries

Establishing and maintaining effective boundaries requires self-awareness, clear communication, and ongoing effort. Healthy boundaries are a pathway from pain to peace, empowering individuals to protect their emotional, mental, and physical well-being while fostering more respectful, fulfilling relationships. Below are actionable steps to implement boundaries in your daily life, facilitating this journey toward peace:

1. **Reflect on Your Needs and Limits:** Before you can set boundaries with others, it's essential to understand your own needs and limits. This self-awareness is key to moving from pain to peace. Spend time reflecting on what makes you feel safe, respected, and valued in relationships. Consider situations where you felt overwhelmed, taken advantage of, or misunderstood. What was missing in those moments? What boundaries were violated? Reflecting on these experiences will help you identify patterns and gain clarity about the boundaries you need to set to protect your peace.

   - Keep a journal to document situations where your boundaries were crossed and how it made you feel, as well as times when confidently asserting your thoughts, feelings, or needs brought a sense of peace and empowerment.

- Check in with yourself daily by asking, "What do I need today?" or "What feels too much for me right now?" This ongoing self assessment helps you stay grounded in your needs and continue moving from pain to peace.

2. **Communicate Your Boundaries Clearly and Assertively:** Effective communication is essential in boundary setting. When you express your needs and boundaries, it is important to do so with clarity and assertiveness. This fosters peace in relationships. Avoid unclear or passive aggressive language, as it often leads to confusion or resentment. Be direct and respectful when expressing your boundaries, remembering that your needs are valid and you are not responsible for how others react. By communicating effectively, you create opportunities for mutual understanding and shared respect, helping to transform pain into peace.

   - Use "I" statements such as, "I feel overwhelmed when I don't have personal time." - Prepare for difficult conversations by rehearsing what you want to say.

3. **Learn to Say No without Guilt:** Learning to say no is a critical aspect of boundary setting and a powerful way to move from pain to peace. Many people feel guilty or anxious when declining requests, especially when they fear disappointing others or being perceived as unkind. However, saying no is an essential act of self-care, protecting your time, energy, and emotional health. It is not an act of rejection but an affirmation of your right to create space for what nourishes your peace.

   - Start small by saying no to minor requests before tackling more significant ones. This helps build confidence in saying no in more significant situations.

   - Use kind but firm language, such as, "I appreciate the invitation, but I need to rest today." or I'm unable to help with that right now but thank you for thinking of me.

Remember saying no is a step toward preserving your well-being, ensure that you protect your peace instead of succumbing to unnecessary pain.

4. **Be Consistent in Upholding Your Boundaries:** Consistency is key to maintaining boundaries and ensuring that they continue to protect your peace. If you are inconsistent in asserting your limits, others may not take them seriously. When you set a boundary, uphold it with respect and persistence. Consistently enforcing your boundaries reinforces your self-respect and encourages others to do the same. This reduces pain and promotes ongoing peace in relationships.

   - If someone repeatedly crosses your boundaries, gently but firmly remind them of your limits. For example, "I've asked that we don't discuss personal topics at work, and I'd appreciate it if we could stick to that."

   Consistently follow through with consequences when necessary to reinforce the importance of your boundaries. For example, if a colleague repeatedly interrupts you during meetings, limit your interaction or set stricter guidelines for communication.

5. **Reassess and Adjust Your Boundaries Regularly:** Boundaries are dynamic and can evolve over time as your circumstances, relationships, and self-awareness change. What once worked may no longer be effective. It's important to regularly reassess your boundaries to ensure they still serve your needs and protect your peace.

   Set aside time every few months to reflect on your boundaries and whether they are still aligned with your needs and current circumstances.

   Ask yourself, "Are my boundaries still protecting my well-being?" and are there new areas of my life where I need to establish limits? This reflection allows you to adjust your boundaries and continue moving from pain to peace.

6. **Seek Support When Necessary:** Setting and maintaining boundaries can be challenging, especially if you have a history of neglecting your own needs or fearing confrontation. Seeking support from trusted friends or mentors who can offer guidance, encouragement, and perspective. Healing from pain to peace often requires external support to help you stay grounded.

   Share your struggles with trusted friends or offer support and validation as you navigate boundary-setting.

   Join a support group or therapy group focused on personal growth, boundary setting, or healing from trauma.

7. **Understand that Boundaries are Mutual:** In healthy relationships, boundaries are not one-sided. Both individuals must honor and respect each other's limits for the relationship to thrive. This mutual respect fosters peace and prevents the buildup of pain. By honoring the boundaries of others, you create a balanced dynamic where both parties feel safe, understood, and valued.

   Setting and maintaining boundaries has far-reaching benefits for both individuals and their relationships. Boundaries create space for mutual respect, emotional security, and personal well-being. They empower individuals to protect their mental and emotional health, reducing stress and resentment while increasing feelings of peace and fulfillment.

   By fostering clarity and consistency in relationships, boundaries help prevent conflict and build deeper, more meaningful connections.

   When we honor our own boundaries and respect those of others, we cultivate a life of balance, confidence, and inner peace. Moving from pain to peace is not just about healing past wounds; it is about actively creating an environment where love, trust, and authenticity can flourish.

   Pay attention when others express their boundaries. Show empathy and respect for their limits, even if they differ from your own.

Ask people about their boundaries directly, especially in new or evolving relationships. For example, "What are your boundaries when it comes to texting or calls?" This helps to avoid misunderstandings and fosters mutual respect.

8. **Be Mindful of Non-Verbal Cues:** Not all boundaries are communicated through words. Pay attention to nonverbal cues such as body language, tone of voice, and facial expressions. These signals can give insight into someone's comfort level and help you navigate situations where they may not be able to vocalize their boundaries. Being mindful of these cues helps you respect the boundaries of others without requiring explicit statements, fostering a deeper sense of peace and understanding.

   - Observe the body language and tone of others when you're interacting with them. If they appear uncomfortable or distant, take a step back and ask if they're okay or if they need space.

   - If someone seems overwhelmed or tense during a conversation, acknowledge it by saying, "I can see this might be too much for you. Let's take a break if you need to."

Healthy boundaries are not just guidelines; they are acts of self-respect and love that allow us to move from pain to peace. By establishing and maintaining boundaries, you pave the way for relationships that are not only healthy but also enriching and enduring.

9. **Set Boundaries Around Your Time and Energy:** Time and energy are finite resources and setting boundaries around how you spend both is essential to maintaining balance. Whether it's saying no to excessive commitments, limiting your availability during certain hours, or being selective about the energy you invest in relationships, setting these boundaries can prevent burnout and emotional fatigue, allowing you to stay grounded and peaceful.

- Be proactive in managing your schedule by setting specific times for work, self-care, and socializing. Let others know in advance when you are and aren't available.

- Practice saying, "I need some time to recharge," or "I'm at capacity right now, so I won't be able to take on that responsibility."

10. **Practice Self-Compassion When Enforcing Boundaries:** It's natural to feel guilty or conflicted when you first begin setting and enforcing boundaries. However, it's important to practice self-compassion during this process. Remember that setting boundaries is an act of self-care, not selfishness, and that you deserve to prioritize your own well-being. When you approach boundary-setting with kindness toward yourself, it becomes easier to navigate difficult situations and preserve your peace.

- Remind yourself that your needs are valid and worthy of respect. When you feel guilty, pause and affirm to yourself, "Setting this boundary is a way to protect my well-being and maintain peace."

- After enforcing a boundary, take a moment to reflect on the decision. Celebrate your courage and acknowledge that you're taking steps to build a healthier relationship with yourself and others.

The Benefits of Healthy Boundaries

Setting and maintaining boundaries has far-reaching benefits for both individuals and their relationships, helping us to move from pain to peace in every area of life. Some of these benefits include:

- **Improved Self-Esteem**: Boundaries affirm that your needs and feelings are valid, which builds confidence and enhances self-worth.

- **Enhanced Communication**: Clear boundaries encourage open and honest dialogue, reducing misunderstandings and promoting peace.

- **Reduced Stress and Burnout**: By saying no to overcommitment and prioritizing self-care, you create space for peace and avoid unnecessary pain.

- **Stronger Relationships**: Respecting boundaries creates a safe space for mutual growth and understanding, leading to deeper and more fulfilling connections.

Remember, setting boundaries is a journey, not a destination. It requires courage, patience, and practice. As you grow in self-awareness and confidence, you'll find that boundaries are not limitations but liberations. They free you to live authentically and connect meaningfully with others. Whether you're healing from past trauma or striving for healthier relationships, boundaries are the key to creating a life filled with respect, harmony, and genuine connection. Through this journey, you can transform pain into lasting peace.

As you embrace the power of boundaries, you're not just setting limits you're laying the foundation for a new way of living. This transformation doesn't end with boundaries; it's the beginning of a greater shift. To truly move forward and create lasting change, it's essential to pair your newfound peace with intentional action.

"Daring to set boundaries is about having the courage to love ourselves, even when we risk disappointing others."
- Brené Brown

Immediate Action

- Identify one boundary you need to set this week and commit to enforcing it.

____

____

____

____

- Practice saying "no" in a situation where you would usually say "yes" out of obligation. Identify those areas and write them down.

____

____

____

____

- Reflect on a recent situation where your boundary was crossed and journal how you can handle it differently next time.

____

____

____

____

Reflection Questions

- What areas of my life need stronger boundaries?

____

____

____

____

- How do I typically respond when my boundaries are challenged?

____

____

____

____

- What steps can I take to communicate my boundaries more effectively?

Example: If I struggle to say no at work, I can practice by setting small limits, such as declining extra tasks beyond my workload, and reinforcing my boundaries with clear communication.

____

____

____

____

Daily Affirmations for Self-Worth: Say These Out Loud With Passion

I am worthy of love and respect. *(Psalm 139:14 AMP)*

My boundaries protect my peace and well-being. *(Isaiah 26:3 AMP)*

I have the right to say no without guilt. *(Galatians 5:1 AMP)*

I am enough just as I am. *(2 Corinthians 12:9 AMP)*

I honor my needs and feelings. *(Proverbs 3:5-6 AMP)*

Setting boundaries is an act of self-care. *(1 Corinthians 6:19-20 AMP)*

I am strong, confident, and capable. *(Philippians 4:13 AMP)*

Heavenly Father,

Grant me the wisdom and strength to set boundaries that protect my peace and well-being. Help me to walk in confidence, knowing that my worth is found in You. As Job 22:21 (AMP) says, *"Now yield and submit yourself to Him [agree with God and be conformed to His will] and be at peace; by this you will prosper and great good will come to you."*

May my relationships be filled with respect and understanding, reflecting Your love.

In Jesus' name, Amen.

CHAPTER 7

Moving Forward: Creating Lasting Change

Setting Goals for Personal Growth and Healthier Relationships

Creating meaningful goals is a crucial first step in the journey toward personal growth and healthier relationships. Begin by identifying specific areas in your life where change is desired be it communication, trust, or emotional support. Using the SMART criteria (specific, measurable, achievable, relevant, and time-bound) can help structure these goals effectively. For instance, instead of setting a vague goal like "be more open," aim for "share feelings with a friend once a week."

Documenting progress and celebrating small victories along the way reinforces motivation and fosters a sense of achievement, nurturing a positive mindset. As C.S. Lewis aptly noted, *"You can't go back and change the beginning, but you can start where you are and change the ending."*

When crafting your goals, break them into manageable steps. For instance, if building trust is your focus, start by identifying one relationship to invest in and create small, achievable actions to strengthen that bond. These incremental changes build momentum and confidence, making larger transformations feel attainable.

Proverbs 16:3 (AMP) states, *"Commit your works to the Lord [submit and trust them to Him], and your plans will succeed [if you respond to His will and guidance].*" This verse reminds us that true success is rooted in aligning our goals with God's wisdom.

The Role of Support Systems in Recovery and Relationship Building

Support systems play a pivotal role in recovery following trauma. Surrounding oneself with understanding and empathetic individuals can provide the necessary encouragement to navigate the complexities of relationship dynamics. Whether through friends, family, or support groups, these connections serve as a safe space for sharing experiences and emotions.

Actively engaging with this network not only aids in healing but also invites constructive feedback, fostering personal growth. For instance, joining a trauma support group can offer the dual benefits of shared experiences and practical advice from those who have faced similar challenges. C.S. Lewis's wisdom resonates here: *"Friendship is born at that moment when one person says to another: 'What! You too? I thought I was the only one.'"* These connections remind us that we are not alone in our struggles and provide the strength to move forward.

Additionally, participating in workshops or therapy sessions can broaden your support system, introducing you to others who share similar experiences and aspirations. Therapy, in particular, offers tools and strategies tailored to individuals, making it an invaluable resource for personal growth and healthier relationships.

Consider creating a "support map "a visual representation of the people and resources in your life. This map can help you identify gaps in your support system and take proactive steps to fill them. For example, if you realize you lack professional guidance, seeking a therapist or counselor can be a transformative addition to your journey.

Ecclesiastes 4:9-10 (AMP) says, *"Two are better than one because they have a more satisfying return for their labor; for if either of them falls, the one will lift up his companion."* This scripture emphasizes the importance of learning on others during difficult times and the strength found in unity.

Sustaining Healthy Habits and Practices Over Time

Creating lasting change requires a commitment to sustaining healthy habits. It is essential to regularly reflect on the progress made and reassess goals as necessary.

Incorporating mindfulness techniques such as meditation or journaling can help maintain awareness of personal growth and emotional states. Building a routine that includes self-care practices, such as exercise, proper nutrition, and social engagement, lays a strong foundation for ongoing well-being.

For example, dedicating 15 minutes each morning to gratitude journaling can shift your mindset and prepare you for the day ahead. Similarly, setting aside time for physical activity, whether it's a brisk walk or a yoga session, supports both mental and physical health.

Forming accountability partnerships with peers can further support consistency in these practices, ensuring that the journey toward healed relationships remains active and evolving. As C.S. Lewis reminds us, *"Isn't it funny how day by day nothing changes, but when you look back, everything is different?"* This highlights the importance of perseverance and daily effort in creating lasting change.

Galatians 6:9 (AMP) encourages persistence: *"Let us not grow weary or become discouraged in doing good, for at the proper time we will reap, if we do not give in."* Consistency in our daily habits leads to long-term transformation.

The Power of Visualization and Gratitude

Visualization and gratitude are powerful tools for sustaining progress and reinforcing positive change. Visualization involves imagining your desired future in vivid detail, helping to clarify goals and inspire action. For instance, envisioning yourself in a thriving, supportive relationship can serve as motivation to cultivate healthy communication habits today.

Gratitude, on the other hand, shifts focus from what is lacking to what is present and good. By regularly expressing gratitude, you nurture a positive outlook and strengthen emotional resilience. Keeping a gratitude journal, where you list three things you are thankful for each day, can foster a sense of contentment and reduce stress. To integrate visualization into your routine, set aside a few moments each day to imagine your goals as if they are already achieved. Pairing this practice with gratitude amplifies its impact, grounding your aspirations in a positive and hopeful mindset.

Philippians 4:8 (AMP) states, *"Finally, believers, whatever is true, whatever is honorable and worthy of respect, whatever is right and confirmed by God's word, whatever is pure and wholesome, whatever is lovely and brings peace, whatever is admirable and of good repute; if there is any excellence, if there is anything worthy of praise, think continually on these things."* This verse aligns perfectly with the practice of visualization and gratitude, guiding us to focus on positive transformation.

Forgiveness as a Cornerstone of Lasting Change

Forgiveness is a cornerstone of creating lasting change. It involves releasing resentment and bitterness, freeing yourself from the emotional weight of past hurts. Forgiveness does not mean condoning harmful behavior but rather choosing to let go of its control over your life.

Begin the process of forgiveness by acknowledging your pain and its impact on your life. Then, make a conscious decision to release that pain and embrace healing. As C.S. Lewis said, *"To be a Christian means to forgive the inexcusable because God has forgiven the inexcusable in you."* This perspective invites us to extend the grace we've received to others, fostering peace and personal growth.

Ephesians 4:31-32 (AMP) reminds us, *"Let all bitterness and wrath and anger and clamor [perpetual animosity, resentment, strife, fault-finding] and slander be put away from you, along with every kind of malice [all spitefulness, verbal abuse, malevolence]. Be kind and helpful to one another, tender-hearted [compassionate, understanding], forgiving one another [readily and freely], just as God in Christ also forgave you."*

Celebrating Milestones and Looking Ahead

Celebrating milestones is an important part of maintaining motivation and recognizing progress. Whether it's achieving a small goal, such as initiating a difficult conversation, or reaching a major milestone, like completing therapy sessions, taking time to acknowledge your achievements reinforces your commitment to change.

Psalm 118:24 (AMP) declares, *"This [day in which God has saved me] is the day which the Lord has made; Let us rejoice and be glad in it."* Each milestone is an opportunity to celebrate God's faithfulness.

In the book of Job, we see a powerful testimony of restoration through forgiveness. Job 42:10 (AMP) states, *"The Lord restored the fortunes of Job when he prayed for his friends, and the Lord gave Job twice as much as he had before."* This illustrates that healing and blessing often follow when we release past hurts and extend grace to others. Like Job, we must trust that our obedience in forgiveness opens doors to restoration and abundance.

Practical steps for forgiveness include writing a letter to the person who hurt you (even if you never send it), engaging in reflective prayer or meditation, and seeking guidance from a trusted mentor or counselor. Over time, forgiveness becomes a transformative act that not only heals wounds but also strengthens your capacity for love and compassion.

Create a system for celebrating your progress. This could include treating yourself to something enjoyable, sharing your success with a friend, or simply taking a moment to reflect on how far you've come. These celebrations serve as reminders that growth is an ongoing process worth investing in.

As Job's story reminds us, restoration is possible. Job 42:12 (AMP) affirms, *"And the Lord blessed the latter days of Job more than his beginning."* No matter how broken our past, God has a plan for our future that is filled with hope, restoration, and peace. Trust that your efforts toward healing will yield fruit in due time.

The process of healing and growth is not linear. There will be setbacks, but each step forward builds strength and fortitude. Take time to revisit the lessons in this chapter regularly as reminders and reinforcements of your journey.

As C.S. Lewis's words remind us, *"There are far, far better things ahead than any we leave behind."* With this hope as your guide, you can step confidently into a future filled with peace, purpose, and possibility.

Remember, this chapter marks not just the end of the book, but the beginning of a new chapter in your life. Take the lessons learned here and apply them with determination and faith. Your journey to peace, fulfillment, and lasting change is yours to claim.

Journal

- Write down three goals that align with your personal growth and relationship-building efforts.

____

____

____

- Identify challenges that may arise and strategies to overcome them.

____

____

____

- Create a visual map of your support system and areas needing strengthening.

____

____

____

- Engage in a guided prayer focused on healing, forgiveness, and transformation.

____

____

____

- Spend five minutes each day visualizing your desired future while expressing gratitude for the progress made.

"I am stepping forward into the life God has planned for me, free from past limitations. My heart is open to healing, and my mind is focused on positive transformation."

Daily Affirmation

Heavenly Father,

I surrender my past and open my heart to the future You have prepared for me. As You say in Isaiah 43:18-19 (AMP), *"Do not remember the former things, or ponder the things of the past. Listen carefully, I am about to do a new thing; now it will spring forth; will you not be aware of it? I will even put a road in the wilderness, rivers in the desert."*

Thank You for the strength to heal, the wisdom to grow, and the faith to move forward. As Philippians 3:13-14 (AMP) reminds me, *"Forgetting what lies behind and reaching forward to what lies ahead, I press on toward the goal for the prize of the upward call of God in Christ Jesus."*

Help me to forgive, to embrace change, and to walk in the purpose You have called me to. I trust in Your words in Jeremiah 29:11 (AMP): *"For I know the plans and thoughts that I have for you, says the Lord, plans for peace and well-being and not for disaster, to give you a future and a hope."*

And just as Napoleon Hill said, *"Whatever the mind can conceive and believe, it can achieve,"* I know that with Your guidance, my thoughts and beliefs are aligned with Your will. Guide my steps and align my heart with Your will.

Amen.

As Napoleon Hill said, "Whatever the mind can conceive and believe, it can achieve."

"The journey from pain to peace is not a destination, but a continuous transformation of the heart, mind, and spirit. As you embrace healing, trust in God's plan for your life and remember, peace comes not from the absence of struggle, but from the presence of faith in the One who makes all things new."

-Danyle

As you reach the end of this journey, take a deep breath and reflect on the transformation that has begun.

You've learned that the road to healing from trauma isn't a straight path. It is a journey of discovering the truth about yourself, your relationships, and the power you hold to create lasting change.

In the chapter on *Navigating Connections After Trauma*, you gained insight into how trauma affects your ability to connect with others, and how healing starts with reconnecting with yourself. By acknowledging the wounds and embracing the healing process, you've laid the foundation for healthier, more meaningful relationships in your life.

In *Understanding Trauma and Its Impact on Relationships*, we explored how trauma infiltrates every aspect of your emotional world, especially how it shapes your interactions with others. But now, with this deeper understanding, you hold the key to transforming these relational dynamics. You can rewrite your story and heal the brokenness by shifting your perspective and choosing to engage in new, healthy ways of connecting.

The chapter on *The Cycle of Negative Thoughts* has empowered you to recognize the patterns that have kept you stuck in the past. You've learned that negative thoughts don't have to control you. With awareness and intentionality, you can rewire your thinking replacing self-doubt with belief, and fear with faith. As you silence the negative narrative, you create space for healing, hope, and peace to flourish.

In *Forgiveness: A Pathway to Healing*, we uncovered one of the most liberating truths: that forgiveness is not just a gift to others it's a gift to yourself. By letting go of the emotional weight you've carried for far too long, you free your heart to experience true peace. You've discovered that forgiveness isn't about excusing past wrongs; it's about releasing the hold they have over your future. With every act of forgiveness, you step closer to the peace you deserve.

Through *Building Healthy Boundaries*, you learned that healing requires protection, not isolation. Boundaries are not walls; they are tools for creating space where you can thrive. With healthy boundaries, you protect your peace, nurture your self-worth, and cultivate relationships that honor your healing process. You've found that true strength lies in knowing when to say yes to what nurtures you, and when to say no to what hinders your growth.

Finally, in *Moving Forward: Creating Lasting Change*, you've learned that healing doesn't end with awareness. It begins with action. Every step you take toward the life God has destined for you is a step toward becoming the person you were always meant to be. You've embraced the truth that transformation is a daily choice a choice to move forward with purpose, passion, and resilience.

As you close the pages of this book, know that your journey is just beginning. The tools, wisdom, and strength you've gathered here are now a part of you. Healing from trauma is not a destination, but a way of living. The peace you seek is already within you.

Trust in the process. Lean into the faith that has carried you this far. The best is yet to come, and with every step you take, you are one step closer to the life of peace, purpose, and joy that awaits.

Sure! Here's a heartfelt and empowering letter to the reader that you can include at the end (or even the beginning) of your book *Pain to Peace: Navigating Connections After Trauma* to encourage ongoing growth and healing:

As you complete this journey, remember that moving forward is a daily commitment. The road to healing and transformation is not a onetime event but a continuous process. Take every lesson you've learned, apply it, and walk confidently into your healed future.

A Letter to You, the Reader

Dear Friend,

Thank you for journeying through these pages with me. It takes courage to face your pain, to sit with your past, and to desire more for your future. If you've made it this far, I want you to know you are already walking in victory. Every step you've taken in this book has been a step toward peace, toward healing, and toward becoming the version of you that trauma tried to silence.

But this is not the end.

Healing is not a one-time decision; it is a lifestyle. The thoughts you choose, the relationships you nurture, and the boundaries you create all shape the life you're building beyond these pages. Let Pain to Peace be your companion. Return to it when the journey feels heavy, when old wounds try to resurface, or when you need a reminder of just how far you've come. This book isn't meant to be read once and placed on a shelf it's a tool for repetition, reflection, and rebuilding.

Use these chapters as a mirror, a journal, a counselor, and a coach. Let them guide you until discipline becomes second nature and a healthy thought life is your new normal. Keep coming back until forgiveness flows more freely, until self-worth is your baseline, and until peace is your permanent address.

You deserve relationships that reflect the love of God, not the lies of trauma. You deserve to thrive in your mind, body, and spirit. So keep pressing forward. Keep practicing. Keep becoming. You are not alone, and you are not finished. This book will be here whenever you need it reminding you that healing is always possible, and peace is always within reach.

With love and expectation,

Danyle Wilson

Welcome to your extended journey of peace
a path overflowing with good things coming out of you,
through you, and to you.
For surely, goodness is chasing after you.

From Pain to Peace:
Prayers, Declarations & Daily Wisdom for Healing and Navigating
Relationships After Trauma

Here are a few sacred tools to guide your heart on the journey to peace, as you learn to love and be loved again after the storm of trauma. These tools are not just stepsthey are soul whispers, helping you rebuild trust, restore connection, and embrace the healing God longs to pour into your relationships. May each one be a light on your path, reminding you that peace is not just possible it is promised.

Proverbs 2:1-10 AMP

My son, if you will receive my words
And treasure my commandments within you,
So that your ear is attentive to [skillful and godly] wisdom,
And apply your heart to understanding [seeking it conscientiously and striving
for it eagerly].
Yes, if you cry out for insight,
And lift up your voice for understanding.
If you seek skillful and godly wisdom as you would silver
And search for her as you would hidden treasures.

Then you will understand the [reverent] fear of the Lord [that is, worshiping
Him and regarding Him as truly awesome] And discover the knowledge of
God.

For the Lord gives [skillful and godly] wisdom.
From His mouth comes knowledge and understanding.

He stores away sound wisdom for the righteous [those who are in right
standing with Him].
He is a shield to those who walk in integrity [those of honorable character and
moral courage],

He guards the paths of justice.
And He preserves the way of His saints (believers).

Then you will understand righteousness and justice [in every circumstance]
And integrity and every good path.

For [skillful and godly] wisdom will enter your heart And knowledge will be
pleasant to your soul.

Today, I declare:

Lord, I receive Your words and treasure Your commands.
My ears are attentive to skillful and godly wisdom.
I apply understanding to my heart, seeking it earnestly and with expectation.

I cry out for insight. I lift my voice for understanding.
I pursue wisdom as I would hidden treasure because You promised that when I do,
I will understand the reverent fear of the Lord and discover the knowledge of God.

You are my source of wisdom, Lord.
From Your mouth comes knowledge and understanding.
You grant sound wisdom to the upright.
Because I walk in right standing with You, you are my shield.

You guard my path of justice and preserve my way.
I walk in integrity with honorable character and moral courage.
I discern righteousness and justice in every situation. Every step I take is guided by integrity.

Because of this, I declare:
Skillful and godly wisdom is entering my heart, *and knowledge is becoming pleasant to my soul.*

Amen.

Scriptures, Prayers and Affirmations

This verse reflects the selfless and sacrificial love that should exist in all meaningful relationships, not only in marriage.

Proverbs 27:17
As iron sharpens iron, so one person sharpens another.
Find someone who will lead you closer to Christ, not into sin.

Ephesians 4:2-3
Be completely humble and gentle; be patient, bearing with one another in love. Make every effort to keep the unity of the Spirit through the bond of peace.
Seek friendships that are humble, gentle, patient, and rooted in love.

Ruth 1:16-17
Where you go, I will go, and where you stay, I will stay. Your people will be my people, and your God, my God.
Build friendships that reflect loyalty and care, like Ruth and Naomi. True friendship involves looking out for one another with compassion and devotion.

Genesis 2:18
Then the Lord God said, "It is not good (beneficial) for the man to be alone; I will make him a helper [one who balances him, a counterpart who is] suitable and complementary for him."

God created us for connection. Healthy friendships offer support, balance, and encouragement aligned with His purpose.

Ecclesiastes 3:14 (AMP)
"I know that whatever God does, it endures forever; nothing can be added to it nor taken from it God does it so that men will fear and worship Him [with awe-filled reverence]."

Lord, what You are doing in me and in my relationships will be lasting. Establish connections in my life that are built on truth, rooted in love, and grounded in Your purpose.
Let every friendship You are forming remain strong, pure, and life-giving for years to come.

I believe my deliverance is not temporary, it is real, complete, and enduring. I declare that I will walk in sustainable healing and wholeness. I declare that I will experience life-giving, trustworthy, and long-lasting relationships divinely appointed and full of peace.
This is my portion. This is my promise. In Jesus' name, Amen.

1 Corinthians 13
A reminder of the power of love: love is patient, kind, and enduring. Love is the foundation of every strong and lasting friendship.

Ecclesiastes 4:9-12
Two are better than one because they have a good return for their labor. If either of them falls, one can help the other up.
Good friends help each other in times of trouble. Healthy friendships provide strength, encouragement, and resilience.

Colossians 3:12-13
Therefore, as God's chosen people, holy and dearly loved, clothe yourselves with compassion, kindness, humility, gentleness, and patience. Bear with each other and forgive one another...
Be compassionate and forgiving. Make room for one another's flaws and extend grace as you grow together.

1 Corinthians 16:14
Let all that you do be done in love.
Lead with love. Be honest, loyal, patient, and compassionate in all your
relationships.

Ephesians 5:25
Husbands, love your wives, just as Christ loved the church and gave Himself
up for her.

Romans 5:19 (AMP)
"For just as through one man's disobedience [his failure to hear, his
carelessness] the many were made sinners, so also through the obedience of
the One Man the many will be made righteous and acceptable to God and
brought into right standing with Him."

It only takes one act of obedience to bring everything into divine alignment.
One yielded heart can shift the course of generations.
Pride kills and destroys relationships of every kind.
But humility heals.
Even when it feels wrong, choose what is right.
That's where peace lives.
And where peace is, restoration follows.

As you embark on this new chapter of your life, choose no longer to respond out of impulse. Instead, give yourself permission to pause. Meditate on the thought or emotion for 24 to 72 hours and watch how your perspective and possibly even your heart begins to shift. Peace often finds us in the stillness before the response. Sometimes, the words you don't speak are the very ones that protect your destiny and preserve your future.

Hush your mouth and save your future." Bishop S.Y. Younger

Philippians 4:6 Amp

Do not be anxious or worried about anything, but in everything [every circumstance and situation] by prayer and petition with thanksgiving, continue to make your [specific] requests known to God.

Breaking Free from Rejection & Abandonment

Lord, we thank You.

Thank You for going deep beneath the surface to excavate every root, residue, and remnant of rejection and abandonment.

We thank You for uprooting every spirit, action, self-sabotaging pattern, emotion, decision, behavior, thought process, and perception that has been shaped by trauma.

Thank You for cleansing the way we see, hear, perceive, and receive information so it is no longer filtered through wounds of the past, but through the clarity of Your truth.

Healing Prayer of Refinement

I declare today: the cycle is broken.
I am no longer bound by the spirit of rejection.
I am no longer chained to the spirit of abandonment.
I am no longer ruled by fear of not being enough, wanted, or chosen.

I surrender every trigger to Your Holy Spirit.
Incinerate the lies. Burn away the strongholds.
Purify my identity, Lord.

As Your Word says in Malachi 3:2-3 (AMP):
"For He is like a refiner's fire and like fullers' soap… He will sit as a refiner
and purifier of silver… so that they may present to the Lord offerings in
righteousness."

I declare:
I am refined.
I am whole.
I am free.
No longer controlled by wounds of rejection or the shadows of abandonment.

I rise in our true identity accepted, loved, and chosen by God. I am not what
was done to me, who I am who you say I am.

In Jesus' name, Amen.

The Quality of Our Faith

1 Peter 5:9–10 (AMP)

"Resist the devil, be firm in your faith [against his attack being rooted, established, and immovable]. After you have suffered for a little while, the God of all grace [who imparts His blessing and favor], who called us to His own eternal glory in Christ, will Himself complete, confirm, strengthen, and establish you making you what you ought to be."

Faith Declaration & Prayer

Father, we thank You that the season of suffering is ending.
Thank You that Your grace is overtaking us with favor and blessing not just for us, but for our families, for generations.

Lord, You Yourself are completing us, confirming what You've spoken over us.
You are strengthening us with power from on high.
You are establishing us making us who we were always meant to be.

Give us the spirit to stand firm in faith when the enemy attacks.
Let our faith be rooted, established, and immovable.
Even when pressure comes, we will not fold.
Even when we feel alone, we remember we are not the only ones suffering.
Others are enduring too, and You are faithful to every one of us.

We declare:

My faith is not flimsy.
My faith is not for show.
My faith is anchored, and it has substance.
I am being made strong, whole, unshakable, and complete.
My faith is not for performance.
*My faith is **anchored in truth, forged in fire, and full of power.***
I am not breaking down we are breaking through.
*I am being made **strong, whole, unshakable, and complete.***
***I** will stand. I will rise. I will endure.*
In Jesus' mighty name, Amen.
In Jesus' mighty name, Amen.

"Wise Men Bring Wealth. Strong Men Keep Wealth."
Apostle Joshua Selman

Financial Breakthrough

Philippians 4:19 (AMP)
And my God will liberally supply (fill until full) your every need according to His riches in glory in Christ Jesus.

Malachi 3:10 (AMP)
Bring all the tithes (the tenth) into the storehouse, so that there may be food in My house, and test Me now in this," says the Lord of hosts, "if I will not open for you the windows of heaven and pour out for you and your household a blessing so great there will not be room enough to receive it."

Proverbs 16:3 (AMP)
Commit your works to the Lord [submit and trust them to Him], and your plans will succeed [if you respond to His will and guidance].

2 Corinthians 9:8 (AMP)
And God is able to make all grace [every favor and earthly blessing] come in abundance to you, so that you may always [under all circumstances, regardless of the need] have complete sufficiency in everything [being completely self-sufficient in Him], and have an abundance for every good work and act of charity.

Wealth with Wisdom & Strength

Father, in the name of Jesus, we declare that we are both wise and strong.
Wise enough to attract wealth. Strong enough to keep it.
You have made us stewards, not slaves to finances.
Our minds are sharp. Our decisions are Spirit-led. Our hands are blessed to build.

We commit our work to You, Lord every plan, every project, every business, every investment.
And because we submit to Your will and guidance, we declare: our plans will succeed.

You, O God, are liberally supplying every need not according to the world's economy, but according to Heaven's riches in Christ Jesus.
Overflow is our portion.
Divine strategy is our portion.
Abundance is our birthright in the Kingdom.

We are not living paycheck to paycheck we are living promise to promise.
We are tithers. We are givers. And You, Lord, said to test You.
So we boldly declare: The windows of Heaven are open over us.
You are pouring out blessings that overflow into our homes, families, businesses, and generations.

Grace is chasing us down.
Favor is positioning us.
Doors are opening, not by force, but by faith.

We are completely sufficient in You.
Not lacking, not scraping, not barely getting by.
We have more than enough for every good work, every need, and every act of generosity.

Wealth with wisdom is our portion.
Strength to multiply and sustain it is our mantle. We receive it, we walk in it, and we testify of it.
In Jesus' mighty name, Amen.

1. Your Purposeful Pursuit

Reflect on your current financial situation:

- What are your current financial goals?
- Where do you see yourself financially in the next 6 months, 1 year, and 5 years?
- How does your financial situation align with the vision God has placed in your heart?

Scripture Reference:

"And my God will liberally supply your every need according to His riches in glory in Christ Jesus." – Philippians 4:19 (AMP)

Vision Statement:

Write a declaration of your financial vision, knowing that God is supplying your every need. What does financial abundance look like for you?

2. Trusting God with Your Finances

Reflection:

- Are you honoring God with your finances? In what areas can you grow in stewardship?
- Are you consistently tithing and giving generously? What has been the impact on your finances and spirit?
- How does your giving align with the purpose God has placed on your life?

Scripture Reference:

"Bring all the tithes into the storehouse, so that there may be food in My house." – Malachi 3:10 (AMP)

Action Steps:

- Commit to bringing the full tithe into God's house.

- Look for opportunities to give in unexpected places. How will you serve others with your wealth?

3. Wisdom and Strategy for Wealth

Reflect on your financial strategies and goals:

- What business opportunities, investments, or career advancements do you feel led to pursue?
- What strategies will you implement to attract wealth and keep it?
- How are you managing your time, skills, and resources to create lasting financial success?

Scripture Reference:

"Commit your works to the Lord, and your plans will succeed." – Proverbs 16:3 (AMP)

Action Steps:

- Identify the key steps needed to reach your financial goals. Break them down into monthly, weekly, and daily actions.
- Seek wise counsel and partnerships that align with your values and purpose.
- Track your progress regularly to stay focused and aligned with your vision.

4. Living in Overflow

Reflection:

- How can you cultivate an attitude of abundance and gratitude, even during challenging financial times?
- How do you plan to use your wealth to bless others and serve God's Kingdom?
- What are some practical ways you can position yourself to experience the overflow of blessings?

Scripture Reference:

"God is able to make all grace come in abundance to you, so that you may always have complete sufficiency in everything and have an abundance for every good work." – 2 Corinthians 9:8 (AMP)

Action Steps:

- Identify areas in your life where you can increase your giving, whether through time, resources, or financial contributions.
- Create a budget that reflects your priorities honoring God, saving, investing, and giving.
- Develop a mindset of abundance and declare that you are a channel of blessings to others.

5. **Accountability and Reflection**:

- How will you track your financial growth and success?
- What metrics will help you measure progress toward your financial goals?
- Who will you share your goals with to stay accountable?

Scripture Reference:

"And after you have suffered for a little while, the God of all grace... will Himself complete, confirm, strengthen, and establish you." – 1 Peter 5:10

(AMP)

Action Steps:

- Create a timeline for achieving your goals, including check-in points to assess progress.
- Seek accountability through a mentor, financial coach, or accountability partner.
- Celebrate each victory, big or small, as you see God's hand of favor on your finances.

6. Affirmation: Declare Your Financial Future

Write your personal declaration based on the scriptures above:

- What do you believe God will do for your finances?
- How do you want to see His blessings unfold in your life?

Father,

We come before You, acknowledging that all wealth, all blessing, and all favor come from Your hand. We commit our financial plans to You, knowing that You will establish them. Help us to honor You with our finances, and as we obey Your word, may we experience the overflow of Your blessings. Thank You for making us wise stewards, strong in faith, and empowered to live in abundance.

In Jesus' name, Amen.

Enlarge our Territory

1 Chronicles 4:10 amp

Jabez cried out to the God of Israel, saying, "Oh that You would indeed bless me and enlarge my border [property], and that Your hand would be with me, and You would keep me from evil so that it does not hurt me!" And God granted his request.

Father, in the name of Jesus,
I/We posture ourselves for greater capacity and higher levels of spiritual power
as we yield fully to You through fervent and effectual prayer.

Enlarge our capacity in the Spirit.
Expand us inwardly, Lord, so we can carry the weight of glory You are
placing on our lives.
Increase our spiritual sensitivity.
Deepen our discernment.
Let us rise with a greater unction and authority in the Spirit.

Stretch our hearts and minds to sustain and multiply divine investments not
merely for personal gain, but as vessels of provision for those in need. Make us
faithful stewards of wealth, wisdom, and divine opportunity.

Enlarge our capacity to obtain:

- *Wealth and resources for Kingdom impact,*
- *Revelation and knowledge of Your Word,*
- *A renewed vocabulary that is no longer bound by the language of rejection, abandonment, or trauma.*
- *We speak from a healed place whole, restored, and redeemed.*

Enlarge our capacity to walk with, serve, and relate to those in elevated
places millionaires, billionaires, government leaders, kings, queens, senators,
presidents, and those assigned to influence nations. Give us uncommon favor
with them not for status, but for service.

Position us to speak, to do business, and to minister among the mighty, with
humility, grace, dignity, and unwavering integrity.

Anoint our speech with eloquence and wisdom.
Clothe us in boldness and confidence fueled by Your Spirit, not our flesh.

Lord, enlarge our capacity to stay rooted in You.
Let us remain anchored no matter the chaos around us, no matter who comes or goes.
Keep us steady in focus, fixed on Your purpose and the divine plan You've assigned to our lives.

We declare: Our territory is expanding.
Our capacity is increasing.
And our lives are positioned to bless others, for the glory of Your name.
In Jesus' name, Amen

Today, I declare:

My God is a generous and faithful Provider.
According to Philippians 4:19, He will liberally, bountifully, and freely supply all my needs.
He fills every lack until full, according to His glorious riches in Christ Jesus not my own strength, but His abundant storehouse.

I bring my full tithe into the storehouse, honoring the Lord with the first fruits of all I receive.
According to Malachi 3:10, I stand on God's promise:
The windows of heaven are open over me and my household.
He is pouring out a blessing so great that there will not be room enough to receive it.

I commit my plans and my work to the Lord.
As Proverbs 16:3 declares, I submit all I do to Him, trusting His perfect wisdom.
Because I align with His will and guidance, my plans will succeed and prosper.

And according to 2 Corinthians 9:8,
God is making all grace, favor, and earthly blessings come to me in abundance.
No matter the circumstance, I have everything I need
I am completely self-sufficient in Him, and I have more than enough for every good work and every act of generosity He calls me to.

I declare I walk in overflow. I live in divine provision.
My finances are blessed, my hands are favored, and my household is covered.
We will lack no good thing, and we are positioned for prosperity spiritually, emotionally, and financially.
In Jesus' name. Amen.

Divine Reset

Based on 1 Peter 4:12-16 (AMP)

"Beloved, do not be surprised at the fiery ordeal which is taking place to test you... But insofar as you are sharing Christ's sufferings, keep on rejoicing, so that when His glory is revealed, you may rejoice with great joy."

Prayer & Declaration:

Father, in the name of Jesus, I thank You for Your promise that through the fiery trials, I am tested, refined, and made stronger in my faith. As I share in Christ's sufferings, I will rejoice, knowing that Your glory will be revealed in me, and I will rejoice with great joy.

Lord, I ask for a divine reset in every area of my life my mind, body, soul, spirit, relationships, dreams, operations, finances, identity, and purpose. Reset the way I walk, talk, and perceive life. Reset the way I see myself and the situations I face. Reset how I show up in relationships, with a heart full of love, humility, and understanding.

Thank You, Lord, for re-establishing me in the newness of life. I receive Your divine reset in my identity and my purpose, establishing my life on a solid foundation in Christ.

I thank You for restoring wealth to me and bringing back divine provision. I declare that as I walk through this reset, my steps are aligned with Your purpose, and You are multiplying everything I put my hands to.

No weapon formed against me shall prosper, and in every circumstance, I will glorify You. Thank You, Lord, for making me worthy to suffer for Your name, for You are with me through it all.

In Jesus' mighty name, Amen.

Time to Give Birth

The Promise of Children(Put your hand on your womb and say this with passion from the depth of your soul)

Isaiah 54:1 (AMP)
"Shout for joy, O barren one, she who has not given birth.
Break forth into joyful shouting and rejoice, she who has not gone into labor [with child]!
For the [spiritual] sons of the desolate one will be more numerous Than the sons of the married woman," says the Lord.

Prayer & Faith Declaration
Father, in the mighty name of Jesus, I thank You that You are the God who watches over Your Word to perform it. I thank You that Isaiah 54:1 is not just scripture it is my reality. I praise You right now as if it is already done, because by faith, I believe it is.

So today, I speak directly to my womb:
Womb, be fruitful.
Womb, open now by the authority of Jesus Christ.
You are no longer barren you are blessed.
You will carry life, you will nurture destiny, you will hold legacy.
Every system, organ, and hormone aligns with divine order.
The blood of Jesus covers you, and the breath of God fills you with life.

I declare that my womb is strong.
I declare that my womb is healed.
I declare that my womb is ready.
The implantation shall happen. The embryo shall grow. The pregnancy shall be full-term, and the delivery shall be victorious.

I cancel every word curse, diagnosis, generational delay, and spiritual attack that tried to close what God has opened.

I silence every voice of fear and elevate my faith in the voice of Truth.

God, You have entrusted me with legacy, and I say YES.

I will mother nations. I will raise revivalists. I will carry glory.

My children are already known in heaven, and now I call them forth into the earth.

And now I boldly declare: I am fruitful.

I am already expecting.

My body is responding.

My womb is alive.

My spirit rejoices.

Heaven has said YES so I align with it.

It is done.

In Jesus' mighty name, Amen.

Scripture:

John 14:12 (AMP):

"I assure you and most solemnly say to you, anyone who believes in Me [as Savior] will also do the things that I do; and he will do even greater things than these [in extent and outreach], because I am going to the Father."

Prayer:

Lord Jesus, as we pursue loving You through prayer, growing in deeper levels of intimacy with You, we continue to believe in the works that You have done healing the sick, raising the dead, healing the lame just by speaking a word and seeing it manifest here on earth.

So be it unto me the same miracles as I continue my pursuit and love for You through prayer and spending time in Your presence.

Continually deliver us from pride and from an arrival mentality, that we may access the power of the age and look like You on this earth.

*Lord, we want a genuine encounter with You an encounter with the God of the Bible that leaves a **provable deposit of** Your Spirit within us, a deposit we can give away as a gift to others.*

*God, give us the ability to **speak and do** as Elijah and Elisha did with **boldness, with authority, and without fear**.*

Declaration:

I walk in miracles, signs, and wonders.
I am delivered from pride and from every false arrival mindset.
I pursue God's presence, and I am filled with a provable deposit of His Spirit.
I move in boldness, authority, and fearless power just like Elijah and Elisha for the glory of Jesus Christ!

Isaiah 26:7 (AMP)

"The way of the righteous [those in right-standing with God living in moral and spiritual integrity] is smooth and level; O Upright One, You make a level path for the just."

Prayer and Declaration

Father, I thank You that according to Your Word in Isaiah 26:7, I am righteous through Christ Jesus, and my way is not steep.
I declare that I will not experience rapid or destructive decline.
I will not be consumed or saturated by wrong influences.
I will not be subject to overwhelming or pervading forces of evil.

My life will not be rough or unstable.
My journey will not be full of stumbling blocks, uneven ground, high grass, or stones of offense.
You, Lord, are my God the One who does what is right and You personally smooth out the path ahead of me.

You are going before me.
You are clearing every obstruction.
You are making the crooked places straight and the rough places plain. You are preparing a path of victory for me.

My journey is steady

My life is saturated with the influence of the Holy Spirit.
I will not stumble.
I will not falter.
I will not fall prey to snares or hidden traps.

I walk in peace.
I am marked by divine progress.
I decree: No rough terrain shall hinder me.

No stone will make me stumble.
No steep decline will swallow my destiny.
The God who goes before me has made the way clear, walking on leveled
paths prepared by the hand of the Almighty.

I am marked by stability.
I am unshaken.
I arise. I walk forward. I possess the land.
And it is so, in Jesus' mighty name. Amen.

Psalm 23:6 (AMP)

"Surely goodness and mercy and unfailing love shall follow me all the days of my life, and I shall dwell forever in the house of the Lord."

I Am Anointed for Good Things ~Bishop S.Y. Younger
Good things are coming out of me.

Goodness is chasing after me.
Mercy is running me down.
I am anointed to produce good things.
I am anointed to build infrastructures.
I am anointed to establish systems.
I am anointed with strategies from Heaven.
I am anointed to have innovative ideas birthed by the Spirit of God.
I am anointed to have witty inventions that bless generations.
I am anointed for blueprints and floor plans that build legacy.
I AM ANOINTED FOR ALL OF IT.

I am going to build recreation centers so the young people in my community have somewhere to go and grow.
I AM GETTING READY TO PRODUCE SOME GOOD THINGS.

Group homes are coming out of me.
There's going to be scholarships in my name that open doors for future leaders.
I'm not only paying for my children's way in school, but I'm going to pay for someone else's children to go to school for all four years.

I AM NOT JUST ANOINTED FOR CHURCH!!!!
Imma bless people in such a way they are going to know there is a real and living God.

I'm about to shift someone's whole destiny because the anointing of Jesus is resting heavily on me.

I AM ANOINTED FOR GOOD THINGS.

MIGHTY DECLARATION:

I decree and declare that I am walking in the fullness of God's promises.

I declare that goodness, mercy, favor, open doors, divine alignments, and abundant resources are overtaking me now.

I decree that strategies, blueprints, and innovative ideas are flooding my spirit, and I am executing them with wisdom and power.

I declare that scholarships, group homes, centers of healing and restoration, and businesses are manifesting through me.

I decree that every seed I sow multiplies and blesses generations after me.

I declare that I am a financier of the Kingdom.

I declare that I am a builder of legacy.

I declare that my hands are anointed to create solutions for my community, my region, and my nation.

I decree that I am a living testimony of the goodness and glory of God on Earth.

GOOD THINGS ARE NOT JUST COMING GOOD THINGS ARE FLOWING OUT OF ME IN JESUS' NAME!

Citations:

Bevere, John. *The Bait of Satan: Living Free from the Deadly Trap of Offense.* Charisma House, 1997.

Munroe, Myles. *Understanding the Purpose and Power of Prayer: Earthly License for Heavenly Influence.* Whitaker House, 2002.

Leaf, Caroline. *Who Switched On My Brain?* Thomas Nelson, 2021.

Nightingale, Earl. *The Strangest Secret.* Nightingale-Conant, 1956.

Hill, Napoleon. *Think and Grow Rich.* The Ralston Society, 1937. *The Holy Bible, Amplified Version.* Zondervan, 1987.

HarperCollins Publishers. *Various Works on Emotional Healing and Personal Development.*

Angelou, Maya. *I Know Why the Caged Bird Sings.* Random House, 1969.

Wigglesworth, Smith. *Manifesting the Power of God.* Destiny Image, 2012.

Collins, Harper. *Emotional Healing and Mental Well-being.* HarperCollins Publishers, Various Years.

American Psychological Association. *"Emotions." APA Dictionary of Psychology,* 2021.

Brown, Brené. *The Power of Vulnerability: Teachings on Authenticity, Connection, and Courage.* Sounds True, 2012.

Hill, Napoleon. *Think and Grow Rich.* The Ralston Society, 1937.

Leaf, Caroline. *Who Switched Off My Brain?* HarperCollins, 2009.

---. *Who Switched On My Brain?* Thomas Nelson, 2009.

Nightingale, Earl. *The Strangest Secret.* Nightingale-Conant Corporation, 1956.

The Holy Bible, *Amplified Version (AMP).* Zondervan, 1987.

Wigglesworth, Smith. *Manifesting the Power of God.* Destiny Image, 2012. Brown, Brené. *The Gifts of Imperfection.* Hazelden Publishing, 2010.

Wolynn, Mark. *It Didn't Start with You: How Inherited Family Trauma Shapes Who We Are and How to End the Cycle.* Penguin Books, 2016.

Scriptural References

"The Book of Job – A Biblical Perspective on Trauma, Resilience, and Restoration."

Matthew 12:34 (AMP): *"For out of the fullness (the overflow, the superabundance) of the heart the mouth speaks."*

Psalm 139:14, 1 Thessalonians 5:18, Jeremiah 29:11, Proverbs 18:21, Philippians 4:8, Romans 12:2 (AMP).

Additional Notes

- Concepts adapted from *Who Switched Off My Brain?* and *Who Switched On My Brain?* by Dr. Caroline Leaf.

- Personal development principles from *Think and Grow Rich* by Napoleon Hill.

- Forward-thinking mindset strategies inspired by *Manifesting the Power of God* by Smith Wigglesworth and the teachings of Earl Nightingale.

  Citation Page: **Biblical References (Amplified Bible, AMP):**

- Proverbs 16:3

- Ecclesiastes 4:9-10

- Galatians 6:9

- Philippians 4:8

- Ephesians 4:31-32

- Psalm 118:24

Books & Authors:

- Hill, Napoleon. *Think and Grow Rich*. The Ralston Society, 1937.

- Leaf, Caroline. *Who Switched Off My Brain?* Thomas Nelson, 2009.

- Nightingale, Earl. *The Strangest Secret*. Nightingale-Conant Corporation, 1957.

Quotes:

- Lewis, C.S. "You can't go back and change the beginning, but you can start where you are and change the ending."

- Lewis, C.S. "Friendship is born at that moment when one person says to another:

- 'What! You too? I thought I was the only one.'"

- Hill, Napoleon. "Whatever the mind can conceive and believe, it can achieve."